FLEET STREET
& THE STRAND

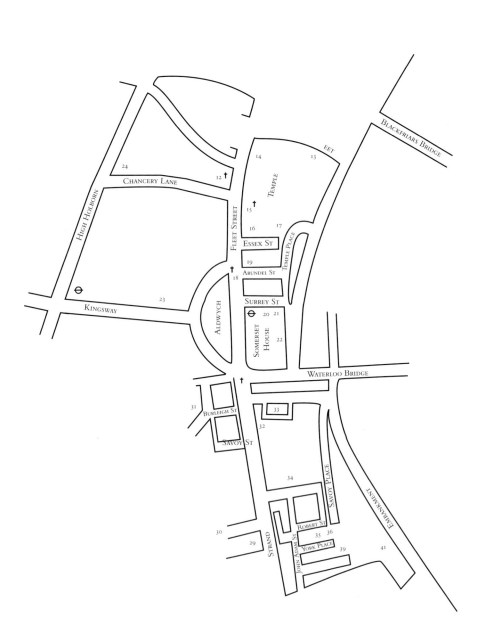

BLACKFRIARS BRIDGE

EET

14   13

Temple

CHANCERY LANE   12 †

24

15 †

HIGH HOLBORN

16   17

FLEET STREET

ESSEX ST

19

TEMPLE PLACE

ARUNDEL ST

18 †

SURREY ST

23

KINGSWAY

ALDWYCH

20 21

SOMERSET HOUSE

22

WATERLOO BRIDGE

†

31

BURLEIGH ST

33

32

SAVOY ST

34

SAVOY PLACE

EMBANKMENT

30

29

STRAND

JOHN ADAM ST

ROBERT ST

35 36

YORK PLACE

39

41

FLEET STREET
& THE STRAND

MALCOLM PARSONS

TEMPUS

For Georgina and David

Cover: The Thames in 1791, showing Somerset House with its watergate for the Controller's barge, the Adelphi and – on the extreme left – the white arch of the York Watergate. Behind this, on the site of York House, is York Buildings, in which Pepys lived.

Frontispiece map: 1-*College of Physicians (Warwick Lane)*, 2-*College of Physicians (Amen Corner)*, 3-Society of Apothecaries, 4-Stationers' Hall, 5-Seacoal Lane, 6-Effigy of Edward VI on Bridewell Gatehouse, 7-St Bride's, 8-Peterborough Court; Poppins Court, Cheshire Cheese, 9-Bolt Court, 10-Gough Court, 11-Crane Court, 12-St Dunstan's in the West, 13-Whitefriars Crypt, 14-*The Mitre*, 15-Prince Henry's Room, 16-The Devereux (*The Grecian – Essex House*), 17-Essex Street steps, 18-St Clement Danes, 19-*Crown and Anchor*, 20-The Old Watch House, 21-The Roman Bath, 22-Somerset House Watergate, 23-*King's College Hospital, Portugal Street*, 24-Staple Inn, 25-Leather Lane, 26-Ely Place, 27-*Old Slaughter's*, 28-Old Charing Cross Hospital (police station), 29-Old BMA House (Zimbabwe House), 30-Bedford Street (*Bedford House*), 31-Exeter Street (*Exeter House*), 32-Peter of Savoy, 33-Queen's Chapel of the Savoy (*Savoy Hospital*), 34-*The Lancet,* 35-Lower Robert Street (*Durham House; Adelphi*), 36-Adelphi Terrace, 37-Of Alley (*York House*), 38-No. 28 Villiers Street (*old Charing Cross Hospital*), 39-Pepys' houses, 40-York Watergate, 41-Camel Corps memorial, 42-No. 36 Craven Street, 43-Bazalgette Memorial, 44-Steps from terrace of *Whitehall Palace*. [Buildings which no longer exist are indicated in italics]

First published 2005

Tempus Publishing Limited
The Mill, Brimscombe Port,
Stroud, Gloucestershire, GL5 2QG
www.tempus-publishing.com

© Malcolm Parsons, 2005

The right of Malcolm Parsons to be identified as the Author
of this work has been asserted in accordance with the
Copyrights, Designs and Patents Act 1988.

British Library Cataloguing in Publication Data.
A catalogue record for this book is available from the British Library.

ISBN 0 7524 3655 4

Typesetting and origination by Tempus Publishing Limited.
Printed in Great Britain.

INTRODUCTION

Visitors studying the history of London do not hurry to visit Fleet Street and the Strand. This is understandable, for apart from some ancient buildings in and around the Temple, Somerset House (a relatively modern structure) and a clutch of interesting churches the overriding impression is one of tawdry shops and deserted newspaper offices. But if, instead of a study of old buildings, history is taken to mean the story of people and events, there are few parts of the city more worthy of attention.

The architectural history of the area falls into four distinct stages. In the Middle Ages the river bank which lay between the western walls of the City at Ludgate and the court at Westminster was relatively deserted. North of the track that was to become Fleet Street and the Strand there was open country – the country of St Giles in the Fields. To the south were the Temple (the one area which has remained relatively unchanged throughout), two palaces (the Savoy and the Bridewell), two monasteries (Blackfriars and Whitefriars) and a line of magnificent town houses belonging to various princes of the Church.

With the Reformation of 1534, the face of London, and in particular of Thames bank, was transformed. Whitefriars and Blackfriars were demolished and the episcopal inns were confiscated or destroyed to provide palaces for greedy courtiers – palaces in which the drama of the later Tudor, the Elizabethan and the Stuart periods was to be enacted.

The era of palaces came to an end in the latter part of the seventeenth century. The population of the hopelessly overcrowded City (i.e. the area within the old city walls – extending roughly from the Tower to a little west of St Paul's Cathedral) was already spilling out into the suburbs and this migration was accelerated by the Great Fire. It could hardly be said that the area was 'going down', for developments in places like Lincoln's Inn Fields and Covent Garden were of a high order, but it was no longer exclusive and the aristocracy, tempted by new mansions near the court at St James's, moved away to Mayfair. The riverside mansions were no longer required and, with the exception of Somerset House (which was rebuilt in 1775), they were gradually demolished. But among the new buildings that appeared in their place were the inns and coffee houses that were to become the haunts of the intelligentsia.

This intellectual activity flourished and by the nineteenth century the area was home to (among other things) the Royal Society and the Royal Academy, various medical clubs, the Royal College of Surgeons, two teaching hospitals, the British Medical Association and *The Lancet*. But the river, once a convenient and pleasant highway for the privileged few who lived along its banks, had become both the main sewer and the water supply of the city. The resulting

9

stench and illness promised to make the area uninhabitable until the problem was solved by the feat of engineering that produced the Embankment.

Over the last 100 years the great institutions have gradually moved away from the area. The press, among the first to arrive some 500 years ago, was one of the last to go, leaving only the lawyers in their inns around the Temple. But among the now tawdry streets one can still find traces of better times – of the artistic pretensions of twentieth-century doctors and of the clubs, dissecting rooms and body-snatching activities of their predecessors; of the cholera epidemics that ravaged the city before the Embankment was built; of the waterside mansions that once opened onto the river; of two royal palaces that were converted into hospitals; of monasteries demolished by Henry VIII and even of Roman pavements and Saxon graves. If only because of these little-known relics, this area is worthy of attention.

Central to this story, therefore, is the array of great buildings that once lay along the bank of the Thames – York House, Durham House, Salisbury House, the Savoy, Somerset House, Arundel House, Essex House, the Temple, Whitefriars, the Bridewell Palace and Blackfriars. But their importance lies not in the buildings themselves but in the events which took place in them or (once they had been demolished) in the buildings which replaced them. The earlier part of this story includes the history of Henry VIII's divorce and of the Reformation; the execution of Edward VI's uncles Thomas Seymour and the Duke of Somerset; Northumberland's attempt to disinherit Mary in favour of his daughter-in-law Lady Jane Grey; the struggle for power between Elizabeth's courtiers Lord Burghley and the Earl of Essex; and the escapades of James I's favourite, the Duke of Buckingham. The latter part follows the reconstruction of the area and the development of many important medical and scientific organisations, two of the greatest building projects ever seen in the city and a medical contribution to the world of art. These events, as will soon be evident, do not lend themselves to neat classification in terms of place, person or time, but by concentrating on the first and by using cross-references I have tried to hold the various strands of the story together.

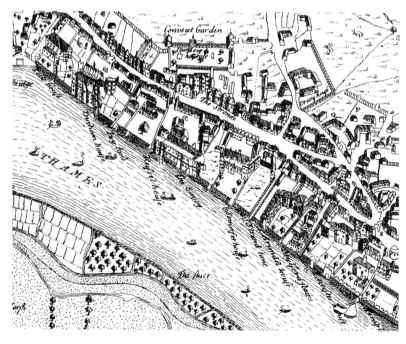

Norden's map of London, 1593.

10

1

CHURCH AND STATE

The Savoy Hospital

Medieval England was dominated by the Church. But the role of the Church was not confined to spiritual matters, for it was heavily involved in government and education, was a leading landowner and employer and provided the medical services of the time. Among these last was England's only attempt to copy the great Italian hospitals of the Renaissance, the Savoy.

Few visitors to London bother to cross Blackfriars Bridge at the end of Fleet Street and look back at the buildings on the north side of the river, for the view is not very inspiring. Behind Cannon Street station one can just see the figure of Justice on the Central Criminal Court, near the spot once occupied by the Fleet Prison. On the other side of the bridge the wedding-cake spire of Wren's St Bride's church peeps out from among its larger neighbours, and further upstream there are the gardens round the Temple. Otherwise the buildings are all relatively new. But before crossing the bridge an observant tourist might have noticed two indications that this is not an area to be dismissed lightly, for on the east side there is the effigy of a corpulent Black

Thames bank to the east of Blackfriars Bridge, showing St. Paul's and Cannon Street station. This area was once occupied by Blackfriars Monastery and Baynard's Castle.

Thames bank to the west of Blackfriars Bridge – the area once occupied by the Bridewell Palace and Salisbury House. The 'wedding cake' spire of St Bride's is to the left of the large building, Unilever House.

Friar and on the west there is the effigy of a king, Edward VI. These opposed symbols of Church and State are the key to the area's eventful history.

The medieval City of London occupied much the same site as the Roman city built 1,500 years earlier. Clustered round the bridgehead that formed the only link between roads running north and south, its buildings huddled within walls set on Roman foundations. On the western flank these had the added protection of the river Fleet, then navigable as far north as Holborn, which joined the Thames at the point where Blackfriars Bridge now stands. Crossing the Fleet was a road that emerged through Ludgate to run along the north bank of the river. To the north, only a few cottages separated it from open country – the country of St Giles in the Fields. On the south, however, it was lined with inns – not inns in the sense of public houses, but inns that were the magnificent town houses of prelates from York, Norwich, Durham, Carlisle, Chester, Worcester, Bath and Wells, Exeter and Salisbury, men whose spiritual (and temporal) powers were such that they could safely live outside the walls of the City.

This road, which was to become Fleet Street and the Strand, was the main overland link between the old City and the Confessor's court and abbey at Westminster. It was a poor structure, and the Tudor description of it as 'very noyous, foul and jeopardous to all people, as well on horseback as on foot' held good long after that time – not that that mattered, for anyone of consequence would make the journey by boat. Yet it was a road that, for many centuries, was to be at the centre of affairs. From an administrative point of view the first section – Fleet Street – was part of the City. Ecclesiastically, however, both Fleet Street and the Strand were in the domain of the abbey.

THE MEDIEVAL CHURCH

The Church seemed indeed to govern almost everything, for the terrified missionaries who had been sent to this war-torn country after the legions had deserted found to their amazement that their administrative ability was prized as highly as their faith. Disciplined, able to read and write, possessed (in Latin) of an international language and being part of an organisation with links throughout Europe, they were in an ideal position to keep records and to assist in government.

Above left: The Black Friar.

Above right: The effigy of Edward VI on No.14 New Bridge Street, the old entrance to the Bridewell.

Part of the medieval London Wall.

This, coupled with their all-important power over the destiny of the souls of men, put the Church in a commanding position. It was a position that it had exploited to the full with the result that, over the years, the bishop had gradually assumed the mantle of the Roman consul. At the same time, because it was customary for wealthy citizens to leave substantial bequests so that masses could be sung for their souls, the Church had become the leading landowner and employer. Some churches had property in as many as 60 parishes and 100 provincial monasteries had land in London. There was Church property on virtually every street within the City, it owned nearly every large building and it received a third of all rents. In all, excluding chapels, there were 126 parish churches and 29 major religious foundations, all of which were constantly being enlarged and beautified. The same was true in the surrounding countryside where, once more, the Church owned vast tracts of land.

This ecclesiastical dominance was clearly visible around the mouth of the Fleet. Just within the walls of the City was the great Dominican monastery of Blackfriars – a community which became very wealthy and influential and which was closely linked with state affairs. Beyond that lay the Fleet, lined with 'houses of office' and stinking so badly that 'the putrid exhalations overcame even the frankincense used in the services, causing the death of many brethren'. On the opposite bank was St Bride's church with its curfew tower and beyond that was Salisbury House, London home of the Bishop of Salisbury. A further twelve abbots or bishops had their homes in surrounding streets – recalled in names such as Ely Place and Peterborough Court and by the carving of a parrot (popinjay) which once marked the home of the Abbot of Cirencester in Poppingaye Court. Beyond Salisbury House was Whitefriars, a second great monastery whose popular Carmelite

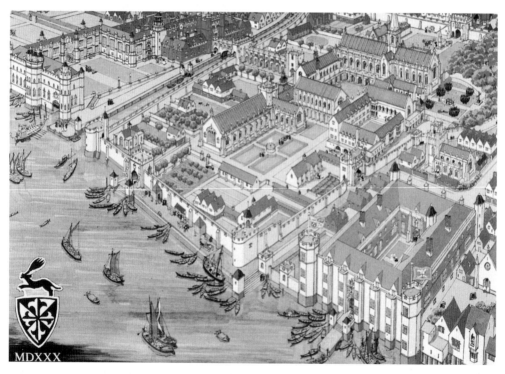

A reconstruction of Baynard's Castle (right), Blackfriars Monastery (centre) and the Bridewell Palace (left). Salisbury House is just visible in the top left-hand corner. (Courtesy of the Worshipful Society of Apothecaries)

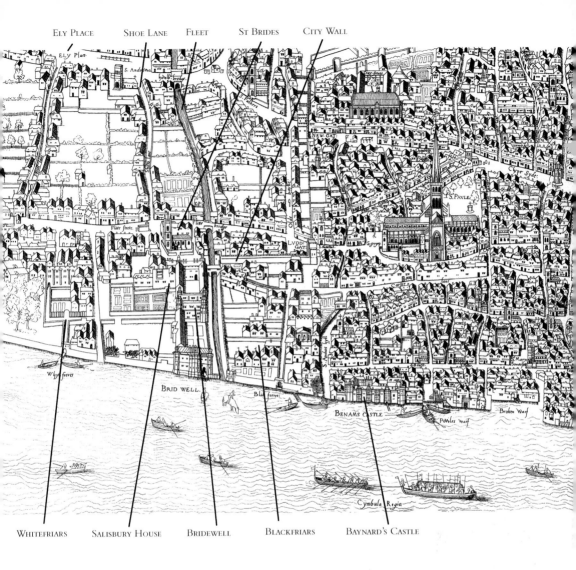

ELY PLACE   SHOE LANE   FLEET   ST BRIDES   CITY WALL

WHITEFRIARS   SALISBURY HOUSE   BRIDEWELL   BLACKFRIARS   BAYNARD'S CASTLE

The copperplate map, 1550. Only three of the fifteen copper plates on which this map was engraved have survived – this one as the 'canvas' for a painting. (Courtesy of the Dessau Gallery)

occupants (unlike most of their colleagues) adhered strictly to their vows of poverty. It extended from Fleet Street to the Thames and from Whitefriars Street to the Temple, and beyond that the line of ecclesiastical inns ran on along the north bank of the Thames to Whitehall. In every respect – spiritual, temporal and economic – it was a community dominated by the Church.

THE ARRIVAL OF THE PRESS

In addition to their spiritual gifts, these clerics endowed the area with three things. The first was the wealth and scholarship that drew the press to Fleet Street. Caxton, whose interests were primarily artistic, had opened his business at Westminster but his successor, Wynkyn de Worde,

15

rightly felt that Fleet Street, being near to this concentration of priests and prelates, had greater commercial possibilities. It also had the advantage, where binding was concerned, of being near to Smithfield and the leather-workers in Leather Lane and Shoe Lane. In about 1500 he therefore moved to the Sign of the Sun opposite St Bride's church, thus forging a link between the Church and the press which is still reflected in the language of the latter. Thus the head of a printers' union is known as the Father of the Chapel, from which errant members can be excommunicated. A printer's boy is known as a devil who, with time, may become a deacon. Type is stored in fonts and lines of print are justified. Black smudges are known as monks and white areas where the print has not taken are called friars. All hark back to a time when, for all practical purposes, only clerics had the wealth to obtain and the skill to use printed material.

THE GUILDS

The second contribution, part religious, part social, was the guilds whose uniformed representatives attend services at St Bride's to this day. Within the Church they cared for individual chapels, providing vestments and candles and employing priests to say masses for the dead. Outside they performed passion plays, paid for schools and almshouses, nursed the sick and buried the dead. By degrees, because those in similar employment often assembled in one area, their little meeting places, forerunners of the village hall, became centres for one or another trade (the shoe- and leather-workers, for example, met in Carmelite House off Fleet Street) and from these groups emerged trade guilds like the apothecaries and barber-surgeons that were to play an important part in the development of medicine.

The medallion of the Guild of St Bride's. (Courtesy of St Bride's church, Fleet Street)

THE SAVOY HOSPITAL

The third contribution of the religious foundations was to the social and medical services of the time. For the poor and needy they were indeed virtually the only source of assistance, and all offered accommodation, outdoor relief and such treatment as was available from the herbarium. Some went further and 'specialised' in particular problems. St Mary Bethlehem (Bedlam) and St Mary Barking, for example, looked after the (barking) mad, while the Priory of St Katherine (which later moved from the site of the dock to the east side of Regent's Park) cared for the terminally ill. Even the Brothers of St Anthony, who collected for those with St Anthony's fire (burning pains and gangrene of the extremities caused by eating mouldy rye bread), had a house in Threadneedle Street. (It was also reputed to have the best school in London, at which Thomas More was educated.) In this way, to use Schama's words, the wider Church became school, theatre, moral tutor, local government and, not least, magic and medicine.

But despite the almost universal presence of religious foundations that provided 'social assistance', hospitals in the modern sense of the word were uncommon. The Strand, however, had one such that is of considerable interest. Count Peter of Savoy, whose statue is above the entrance of the Savoy Hotel, was the uncle of the wife of Henry III and a favourite of the King – so much so that he was given the Savoy Palace, one of the finest dwellings in London. He put it to good use, 'lodging there many beautiful ladies from the courts of Europe whom he married to rich young English nobles'. On his death it passed in turn to the Black Prince and then to John of Gaunt before being virtually destroyed in Wat Tyler's rebellion of 1381. Thereafter it remained derelict until 1505, when Henry VII started to become concerned about the shortage of 'acute beds' in London. Finding little support in England, he looked for advice

Peter of Savoy.

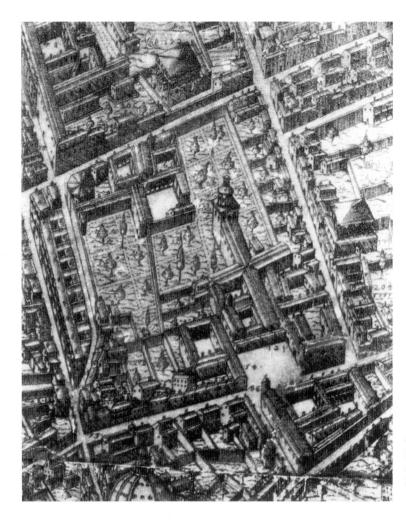

Santa Maria Nuova Hospital, Florence. (Courtesy of SCALA, Museo di Firenze, 1990)

to the Continent, where the planning of such buildings was taken more seriously. As early as 1452, for example, a treatise by Alberti had recommended that male and female patients, patients with acute and with chronic disorders and those who were infectious should be housed apart. Yet it was almost by accident that developers enlarging the tiny Santa Maria Nuova Hospital in Florence produced a cruciform building, ideally suited for this purpose. The wards were light and airy and the patients were easily kept under observation. Different sorts of patients could be segregated in the various wings of the building and the altar – an essential piece of 'equipment' – could be set in the intersection where it was visible to all. The design was therefore copied, reaching its zenith in the great Ospedale Maggiore in Milan.

The hospital in Milan was seen and admired by several English visitors, but was only replicated in England in Henry's Savoy Hospital. This building was dedicated to St John the Baptist (popular with surgeons because water from the Jordan was said to staunch wounds), whose statue stood over the gateway from the Strand. It was 280ft long and 220ft across the transepts. There were 100 beds and each bedstead, which cost the enormous sum of 20 shillings, was fitted with a chest and curtained all round. The coverlets and the gowns of the staff bore the Tudor rose and the glass and plasterwork were of royal quality. At a time when few dedicated hospitals were being

Savoy Hospital. (Courtesy of the Guildhall Library, London)

built in England, and none of this standard or to this design, it was of outstanding importance. Along with St Bartholomew's, St Thomas's and St Mary Spital it was almost certainly one of the buildings that Thomas More had in mind when he envisaged for his Utopia a hospital service for the sick and not mere hospices for the disabled:

> In the circuit of the citie a little without the walls they have four hospitalles, so big, so ample and so large that they may seem like four little towns ... they were devised of that bigness partly to the intent that the sycke, be they never so many in number, should not lie in throng ... and partly that they which are taken and holden with contagious diseases such as would by infection crape from one to another might be laid apart from the company of the residue. These hospitalles be so well appointed with all things necessary to health ... and the diligent attendance through the continual presence of cunning physicians ... that no sick person in all the citie had not rather lie there than in his own house.

It was a vision that had so nearly been fulfilled and that was about to be destroyed.

2

THE REFORMATION

The Bridewell Palace, Blackfriars and Whitefriars

The validity of Henry VIII's first marriage was (unsuccessfully) challenged in hearings at Blackfriars and the Bridewell Palace, and the subsequent break with Rome resulted in the wholesale confiscation and destruction of Church property. The social and medical services of the City were destroyed and it was with some difficulty that five hospitals were restored.

In 1501 Prince Arthur, elder son of Henry VII, married the Spanish princess Catherine of Aragon. The wedding was held in St Paul's Cathedral and the banquet which followed took place in Baynard's Castle, the recently rebuilt home of the House of York which stood to the east of Blackfriars. It was an area to which, over the following years, Catherine was to make two further important visits.

The marriage was a disaster. Within six months Arthur was dead and for the next seven years his sixteen-year-old widow, isolated in a foreign country, eked out an impoverished existence in Durham House while her father and her father-in-law haggled about her future. Then, within six weeks of the death of Henry VII, her fortunes were transformed as she married his heir, Henry VIII (1509-1547). This was a match which owed as much to genuine affection as to political expediency, for Catherine was an attractive, well-educated, intelligent woman. But it was a marriage which required papal dispensation, for it was within the degrees of affinity prohibited by the Church.

Twelve years later, in 1522, Catherine had the all too rare pleasure of a visit from a relative, her nephew the Emperor Charles V. In part this was a further attempt to trim the balance of power between England, France, Spain and the Empire. But it was also an attempt to sort out a looming dynastic problem, for after a series of obstetric disasters the queen, now thirty-five years old, had only produced one surviving child, Princess Mary (who, along with Prince Arthur, was tutored by the scholarly Thomas Linacre, first president of the College of Physicians). Year by year the prospect of a male heir was diminishing, and as an alternative it was proposed that Mary should be married to the Emperor. This meeting took place in another mansion which had just been rebuilt, the Bridewell Palace. There had been a royal residence on the west bank of the Fleet for over 500 years but latterly it had fallen into decay and much of the western part of the site had become the London home of the Bishop of Salisbury. In 1515, however, following a fire at Whitehall, Henry decided to rebuild the Bridewell, and its three courtyards now sprawled along the west bank of the Fleet opposite Blackfriars. This work had not been completed when Charles arrived, and for this reason he was housed in the monastery opposite – a private bridge with a gallery lined with tapestries being built for his convenience.

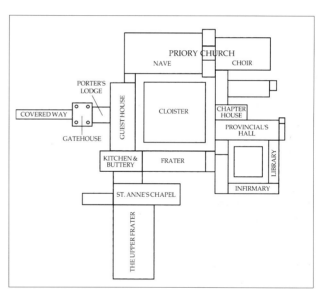

Above: The mouth of the Fleet with the Bridewell Palace on the left and Blackfriars on the right.

Right: Plan of Blackfriars Monastery. The covered way which leads to the bridge from the Bridewell Palace and the guest house used by Emperor Charles V became the Hall of the Worshipful Society of Apothecaries. The frater in which Henry's divorce hearing was held became a playhouse. (Courtesy of the Worshipful Society of Apothecaries)

Sadly, it soon became evident that from Charles' point of view the proposed marriage had one serious disadvantage. In an uncertain world he was under pressure to produce an heir, and the Princess Mary was still only six years old. To the dismay of Catherine, who longed for this further link between the two families, and to the fury of the King, the agreement was broken and Charles looked elsewhere for an older bride. Soon after this, Henry's yearning for a male heir, his roving eye and/or a feeling that marriage to his brother's widow might after all have been illegal caused him to seek a papal annulment of his marriage. The timing, however, was inopportune, for Charles had just seized Rome and, all other considerations apart, it was unlikely that the Pope would allow Henry to divorce his captor's aunt. Nevertheless, in 1529 a hearing was convened at Blackfriars and the Bridewell.

This was an area that the papal legates appointed knew well, for Wolsey had once held the living at St Bride's and Campeggio, in addition to being Archbishop of Bologna, held the bishopric of Salisbury, whose London inn was Salisbury House. The hearings took place in the Bridewell Palace and in the frater of Blackfriars, which the participants were able to reach via the private bridge built for Emperor Charles V. The queen, however, was housed in Baynard's Castle, where her ill-fated marriage to Prince Arthur had been celebrated. The argument dragged on for months, but instead of producing a verdict it was decided that the case should be referred back to Rome. Henry was furious, Wolsey was dismissed and after a violent argument with Catherine at a dinner in the Bridewell Palace on 30 November 1529 the King stormed out of the room.

Meantime Henry's inamorata Anne Boleyn, her father and an obscure cleric called Cranmer had repaired to Durham House where they adduced evidence that convinced Henry – himself no mean theologian – that as head of state he was also head of the Church and that the matter therefore rested in his hands. As a result Henry, Defender of the Faith, abrogated papal control

The hearing before Cardinals Wolsey and Campeggio. (Courtesy of the Guildhall Library, London)

and unleashed an orgy of looting and destruction that was to alter the very face of London. Visitors reported that what had once been a city of palaces and Roman remains had become 'a city of ruins – ruins everywhere – ruins of cloisters, halls, dormitories, courts, chapels, churches and hospitals'. The ecclesiastical buildings round St Bride's suffered badly. The frater of Blackfriars, in which the validity of Henry's marriage had been considered, became an indoor theatre in which Shakespeare's company from the Globe, the King's Men, performed during the winter months; for this reason the area is now known as Playhouse Yard. The guest house and part of the covered way from the Bridewell came into private hands and in 1632, when the apothecaries finally broke free from their demeaning association with the grocers, they were taken over as the hall of the new guild. Evidently the stench from the Fleet persisted, for as Samuel Garth sneeringly observed in his poem 'The Dispensary':

> Here where Fleet Ditch descends in sable Streams
> To wash the sooty Naiads of the Thames
> There stands a structure rising on a Hill
> Where Students take their licence out to kill.

Salisbury House passed to the Sackville family (later the Earls of Dorset) and the buildings and land of Whitefriars were granted to the royal physician, William Butts.

William Butts who appears as one of three figures on one side of the King on the picture of Henry VIII presenting a charter to the newly founded Guild of Barber Surgeons – a painting which Pepys attempted to buy – was clearly a man of some importance. He was sent to care for

Above left: The Hall of the Society of Apothecaries. (Courtesy of the Worshipful Society of Apothecaries)

Above right: Dr William Butts. (Courtesy of the Royal College of Physicians)

Anne Boleyn when she developed the sweating sickness – a condition which killed her brother-in-law – shortly before her wedding. He looked after Henry's precious son when, in infancy, he became seriously ill. And it was to him that the King gave graphic details of the manner in which the body of the unfortunate Anne of Cleves was 'so disordered and indisposed' that it 'could not excite or produce lust in me'. But his services went beyond the field of medicine. Butts had been trained in the evangelically inclined Gonville and Caius College, Cambridge and was used by Anne Boleyn (who had similar sympathies) to channel funds to Lutheran scholars at a time when such activities were not without risk. He is also portrayed by Shakespeare protecting the reformist Cranmer from the plots of Cromwell and the 'Catholic' bishops (*Henry VIII*, Act V, scene ii), and because of such activities he is mentioned with favour in Foxe's *Book of Martyrs*. Later on he was instrumental in introducing Protestant scholars like John Cheke and Richard Ascham – whose teaching moulded the mind of the young Edward VI – and William Cecil (later Lord Burghley), who began his career as secretary to the man who was to become 'Protector' Somerset (see pages 44-45).

Although the great hall of Whitefriars survived for a time as a theatre, the majority of the building was demolished, 'yielding many fine houses' – one of which was still owned by Butts at the time of his death. Eventually, however, with the exception of the names of Carmelite Street and Whitefriars Street, it seemed that all traces of this monastery had vanished. This, in fact, was not quite true, for in 1895 an agent engaged to sell a house behind St Bride's discovered a curious underground cellar that was full of rubbish. Closer examination revealed that it was a room about 12 feet square which had two doorways and a ribbed stone ceiling that rose up to a dome. It proved to be a fourteenth-century crypt, 'a gem of its kind' according to the archaeological survey, that had once been under the prior's house of Whitefriars Monastery. This structure, which was moved during the construction of an office block halfway down and to the west of Whitefriars Street, can still be seen in the basement and is virtually the only relic of the mass of ecclesiastical buildings which once clustered around St Bride's. (The vaults of the north gatehouse are said to exist under the Cheshire Cheese at the north-east end of Fleet Street.)

The crypt of Whitefriars Monastery in Britton's Court, Whitefriars Street. (Courtesy of the Guildhall Library, London)

The destruction in the surrounding streets was every bit as great. The homes of the Bishops of Glastonbury, Lewes, Malmesbury, Peterborough and Cirencester became inns called the Dolphin, the Walnut Tree, the Castle, the Bell and the Popinjay, and the episcopal mansions along the bank of the Thames towards Whitehall were either taken over by courtiers (like York House, Arundel House and Durham House) or demolished to make way for the new palaces of the Earls or Dukes of Essex and Somerset. To build his mansion, Somerset alone was said to have demolished the Strand Inn (one of the Inns of Chancery), the houses of three bishops, two churches and the cloisters of St Paul's, dumping unwanted human remains in unhallowed ground outside the city walls. It was an unfeeling act that the populace did not forget when, a few years later, he fell from grace.

THE AFTERMATH

In some instances, the new owners of Church property obtained more than land and building material. The great religious houses had had the right to protect fugitives from summary justice because the ground on which they stood was, by tradition, outside the jurisdiction of the City. The sites retained this immunity, and as the aristocracy scrambled to obtain building material others availed themselves of this intangible asset. Dutch watchmakers set up business beyond the reach of the guilds in St Martin's le Grand, the home of the Bishop of London became a haven for debtors and the (unqualified) apothecary Culpeper worked on the site of the old Spitalfields Hospital. The monastery of Blackfriars became an artists' colony and it was here that the Master of the Revels set up London's first indoor theatre. But south of Fleet Street, around Whitefriars, a more sinister change took place. Following the destruction of the old monastery, unfortunates on the fringes of society and those seeking sanctuary from the law were left without material support. The site, however, retained its immunity and it rapidly became a refuge for the dregs of society. Its occupants paid no taxes, refused to clean the streets and defied authority. Known as Alsatia (after the territory of Alsace which, for many years, was a disputed frontier), it became a notorious haunt of criminals (both real and fictional) from which officers of the

SOMERSET HOUSE ARUNDEL HOUSE ESSEX HOUSE TEMPLE WHITEFRIARS BRIDEWELL BLACKFRIARS BAYNARD'S CASTLE

Visscher's panorama of London (1616) from Somerset House to St Bride's.

watch were promptly and violently ejected. Among its many inhabitants were Moll Cutpurse, a young woman 'beyond the control of her family' who became a notorious 'fence' and was eventually buried in St Bride's, and Daniel Defoe who, while hiding here from his debtors, got the inspiration for his book *Moll Flanders*. Over the years numerous unsuccessful attempts were made to control these 'rogues, vagabonds and sturdy beggars', but it was not until the end of the eighteenth century that they met with some measure of success.

HOSPITAL SERVICES

The effect of the Reformation on the social and medical services of the City was even more devastating as the religious foundations, deprived of both income and premises, had no option but to discharge their 'patients'. The blind inmates of St Mary Without Cripplegate, for example, were simply 'thrown out to stumble along and beg' and the streets were soon crowded with 'pore, sicke, weake and sore people of the City and poor wayfaring people repairing to the same'. At the same time, three of the four great hospitals were closed and the activities of St Bartholomew's were greatly curtailed. To those intimately involved, the extent of this disaster was immediately apparent, but when the Lord Mayor, Sir Richard Gresham, sought permission to take over the running of St Thomas's in 1540 his request was refused. An offer to buy the four great friaries for 1,000 marks was contemptuously dismissed as 'penny-pinching' and although Greyfriars was eventually sold to the City, other buyers were found for Blackfriars, Whitefriars and Austin Friars.

As was inevitable, the situation continued to deteriorate and by 1544 the King was forced to participate in the 're-founding' of St Bartholomew's. Three years later Gresham managed to purchase the site of St Mary Bethlehem (Bedlam) as an asylum and in 1551 Edward VI allowed St Thomas's to be reopened by the City under the less offensive patronage of St Thomas the Apostle. By 1553 an orphanage for 400 children (Christ's Hospital) had been established on the site of Greyfriars Monastery and in the same year the great Bridewell Palace, 'which we did no longer like on account of the fylthy stynkyng dytch [the Fleet river] which runneth along the side of it', was handed over as a 'hospital for all idle rogues who need correction'.

The Bridewell was obtained as a direct result of a sermon, preached before Edward VI, in which Bishop Ridley daringly pointed out the contrast between the palaces of the nobility and the poverty, starvation and crime that raged outside their doors and in the ruins of the monasteries and churches they had ravished. He therefore had good reason to feel alarmed when he was ordered not to leave the building after the service. In fact he was granted a long private interview with the young King, who had taken careful notes of the sermon and was now asking for more specific instructions. In seeking permission to use this building, Ridley, who was shortly to be martyred in Oxford, hoped mainly to organise the training and reform of those who, for want of employment, had fallen into 'that puddle of idleness which is the mother of all beggary and mischief'. But this lofty ideal was never realised and the Bridewell, which rarely contained more than about 150 inmates, eventually became little more than a prison from which, on occasions, recruits were sent to the Army and batches of orphans were sent 'to populate Virginia'. On rather dubious legal grounds, its officers were required to round up 'rogues, beggers, strompets and pylfering theves', to eject those who lived elsewhere and to hand the remainder over for 'correction'. Other inmates were sent there for interrogation and punishment by torture, and Shakespeare's line 'I'll manacle thy neck and feet together' (*The Tempest*, Act I, scene ii) could well be a reference to a device which was in use at least until 1598. The building was destroyed in the Great Fire but was rebuilt, and was eventually demolished in 1864, the occupants having been sent to Holloway. During excavations for the Keyser Royal

Hotel (which stood on the site now occupied by Unilever House), a series of brick arches from the old building was discovered, but the only visible relic of the building that remains is an effigy of Edward VI that commemorates his gift and forms the keystone to No. 14 New Bridge Street, the old entrance to the Bridewell.

Above: A ward in Bridewell Hospital. (Courtesy of St Bride's church, Fleet Street)

Right: The old entrance to the Bridewell, No. 14 New Bridge Street.

The Savoy Hospital, meantime, had fallen on hard times, becoming 'a lodging for loiterers, vagabonds and the dissolute who lie all day in the fields and at night are harboured there, which is rather the maintenance of beggary than any relief of the poor'. In 1553 its endowments were therefore handed over to a collective consisting of St Mary Bethlehem, St Thomas's, the Bridewell and Christ's Hospital. This group was later joined by St Bartholomew's to form an association known as the Royal Hospitals, which lasted until 1587. By this time (in 1556) Mary had refounded the Savoy, but it was never a success. Indeed in 1582, when an enquiry was ordered after the Queen's coach had been surrounded by a group of vagrants, it was deemed to be 'the chief nurserie of all these evell people'. It served as a military hospital during the Civil War, became a barracks in 1679 and was eventually destroyed by fire in 1776. The ruins were cleared in 1815 to make way for Waterloo Bridge and all that now remains of one of England's greatest hospitals is the (much restored) Queen's Chapel of the Savoy, headquarters of the Royal Victorian Order.

In conclusion, it is perhaps only fair to mention that in other cities the influence of London's great benefactor, Sir Richard Gresham, was less benign. During the depredation that followed the Pilgrimage of Grace, he bought Fountains Abbey, most of its estates and some 400 Church properties in York, and impoverished that city by transferring the income from these sites to London.

The Queen's Chapel of the Savoy, the only relic of the Savoy Hospital.

3

ESSEX (LEICESTER) HOUSE

The history of Essex House, once the home of the Bishops of Exeter, is typical of the great Thames-side mansions. Its new owners, who patronised poets, playwrights and the 'new learning', were also heavily involved (often with the assistance of their medical attendants) in political rivalry, espionage, rebellion and murder. The house was eventually demolished by a doctor turned property developer and was replaced by – among other things – a coffee house frequented by members of the Royal Society.

As the great houses along the Thames fell into the hands of the nobility, episcopal serenity gave way to political drama. The mansion of the Bishops of Exeter, which stood to the west of the Temple, became the home of the Earl of Essex. Here, amid a cast of poets and philosophers, dramatists and magicians, spies and sodomites, he conducted his struggle to replace Lord Burghley as the Queen's adviser – a battle that culminated in armed insurrection, defeat and death.

The latter part of the sixteenth century was a period of national and international tension. The Protestant countries of northern Europe had rebelled against the corrupt Catholicism of the south, and reforms subsequently instituted by the Jesuits left two groups of religious fanatics at loggerheads. Nowhere was this more evident than in the Low Countries, traditional trading partners of England and one of Spain's most valuable possessions, which had rebelled against the imposition of taxes and papist doctrines.

In theory, England was not involved in these conflicts, for after a period of extreme turbulence a Protestant regime had been established and, despite raids on Spain and the Low Countries, the nation was not at war. But the 'old faith' was by no means dead and as Elizabeth (1558-1603) had no direct heir, the Catholic Mary Queen of Scots was a potential successor. Assisted perhaps by assassination or invasion, a return to Catholicism was therefore a distinct possibility. Spain, indeed, was dedicated to this ideal – an eventuality which newly ennobled Protestant courtiers such as Lord Burghley (William Cecil), Sir Nicholas Bacon and Sir Francis Walsingham were intent on preventing at all costs. Trained in law, this close-knit group formed an embryonic civil service. Its members were highly cultured, for Burghley and Bacon had both married daughters of Sir Anthony Cooke, the tutor who introduced Edward VI and Elizabeth to the 'new learning', and this was reflected in the intellectual development of Burghley's nephews, Anthony and Francis Bacon, and of his wards, who included the Earl of Southampton and the young Earl of Essex. Yet within this group there were also divisions, for Burghley, whose intention it was that he should be succeeded by his son Robert Cecil, believed that the Spanish threat should be met

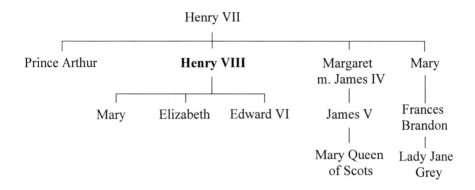

Table 1. Henry's potential heirs. (To simplify matters many of the following tables are incomplete and children are not always shown in order of birth.)

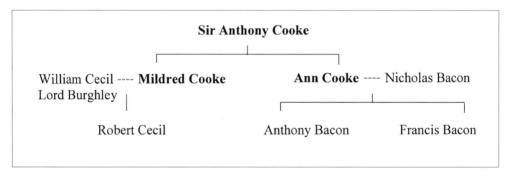

Table 2. The Cooke/Burghley/Bacon dynasty.

by harassment rather than by direct action. Essex, by contrast, favoured outright war, and the intense rivalry that developed between him and Lord Burghley was to have fatal results for more than one of the occupants of Essex House.

ROBERT DUDLEY, EARL OF LEICESTER (1532-1588)

Essex House stood between the Middle Temple and Milford Lane, on land which was originally the Outer Temple of the Knights Templar. Once the inn or town house of the Bishops of Exeter, it was seized by Henry during the Reformation and by 1563 had passed into the hands of Robert Dudley, Earl of Leicester, who virtually rebuilt it. Dudley was a son of the Duke of Northumberland, who had been executed for trying to displace the Catholic Mary with the Protestant Lady Jane Grey (see page 97) and it was for this reason that, on her accession, Elizabeth asked him to arrange her coronation. This was a delicate matter, for the nation was not accustomed to being ruled by queens. Moreover, Elizabeth was the daughter of Anne Boleyn, whose marriage to Henry had occasioned the break with Rome, and in some circles it was even

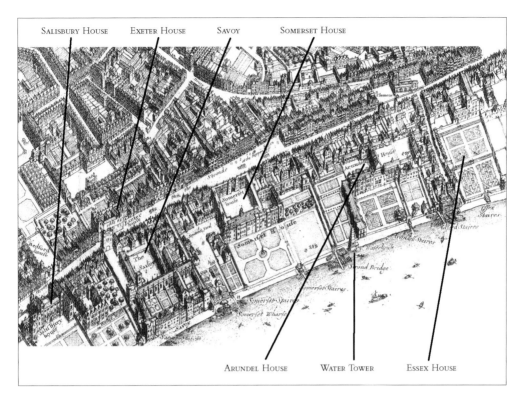

SALISBURY HOUSE   EXETER HOUSE   SAVOY   SOMERSET HOUSE

ARUNDEL HOUSE   WATER TOWER   ESSEX HOUSE

Hollar's view of London (1658). Note the cruciform Savoy Hospital and the water tower near the gallery running down from Arundel House. (Courtesy of the British Museum)

rumoured that Henry was not the father. In a country where many still hankered after the 'old faith' and in the face of dire warnings from the likes of Calvin and John Knox, her accession did not therefore command universal support, and it was essential that the coronation ceremony should be flawless.

Under the circumstances, Leicester's choice of an assistant was surprising. Dr John Dee, one of the outstanding intellects of his time, was among those who struggled to introduce the 'new learning' from the Continent (see page 97). A great bibliophile and an expert on cryptography, mathematics, cartography, navigation, astronomy, astrology and magic, he had been the tutor of Philip Sidney and of the sons of the Duke of Northumberland and the Earl of Pembroke. During Mary's reign, he and his associates had initially been persecuted, but Dee then reappeared as assistant to the much-hated Bishop of London. He was indeed vilified as 'Bonner's chaplain' in Foxe's *Book of Martyrs* (published in an abbreviated form by Dr Timothy Bright) although his name – unlike that of many others – vanished from later editions. He now appeared once more, not only to select a suitable day for Elizabeth's coronation but also as her 'magician' and the adviser to the many navigators of her reign. It seems probable, therefore, that he had in fact served as one of her secret agents during the previous reign.

The Earl of Leicester was among the most powerful and colourful of Elizabeth's courtiers. He courted the Queen and there was a strong suspicion that the 'accidental' death of his first wife was engineered to make way for a marriage. Nor was this the only occasion on which he, his medical attendants or his thugs were thought to have 'eliminated' opponents. It was, for example, most convenient that Lord Sheffield should die soon after he discovered that Leicester was having an affair with his wife. But the most notorious incident of this sort concerned Lettice, the glamorous wife of the first Earl of Essex. Lettice was not the first member of her family to deploy her considerable charms to her advantage, for she was the granddaughter of Mary Boleyn, Anne's sister and another of Henry's conquests (Henry was reputed to have enjoyed the favours of both sisters and of their mother, although he denied the latter). Her ill-concealed affair with Leicester infuriated the Queen who, while not intending to marry Leicester herself, was equally determined that nobody else should enjoy his company (except, that is, for Mary Queen of Scots, who she planned to bring under English control by marrying her to the Earl; Mary and Leicester, however, had other ideas). Nevertheless, while Essex was campaigning in Ireland (an expedition which Leicester, as a Privy Councillor, took pains to prolong), the romance flourished. And when the Earl died an unpleasant death in Dublin Castle, it was widely rumoured (despite post mortem evidence to the contrary) that he had been murdered. Two years later his widow was pregnant and, although Leicester claimed that the pair had been married in secret, her enraged father insisted that the ceremony should be repeated before impeccable witnesses. This of course angered the Queen, whose fury was not lessened by the ostentatious behaviour of the bride, and Leicester found for a time that it was advisable to stay away from the court.

ROBERT DEVEREUX, SECOND EARL OF ESSEX (1566-1601)

After the death of his father, Robert Devereux, second Earl of Essex, became a ward of Lord Burghley. But because Burghley wanted his son Robert Cecil to inherit his political power, his wards and nephews (the Bacon brothers) were driven out of Burghley (Exeter) House, which stood on the site now occupied by the Strand Palace Hotel, and left to fend for themselves. This allowed the second Earl to establish a rival 'power base' at Essex House. Unlike his stepfather the Earl of Leicester, Devereux had distinguished himself during the war in the Low Countries, although he was not particularly successful as a military commander. Indeed, one of his most significant acts was to loot the library of the Bishop of Faro, a small Spanish town from which the defenders had already moved everything else of value, and give the books to his protégé Thomas Bodley, who subsequently used them to form the nucleus of the Bodleian Library at Oxford. Nevertheless, dramatic gestures like hurling his lance into the gates of a besieged city and challenging the governor to single combat captured the public imagination, and Philip Sidney, Leicester's nephew and Essex's patron, bequeathed his sword to his charismatic but unstable disciple as an indication that Essex was to inherit his image. The elegant but penniless teenage Earl rapidly became a favourite at court, and was for a time a suitor of the ageing queen. But this absurd affair soon came to an end, and Essex married Sidney's widow, Walsingham's daughter Frances.

Using his influence at court to recruit and reward disciples, Essex established at Essex House a new power base from which to challenge the authority of the now ageing Burghley. It was a centre strongly influenced by the memory of his mentor Philip Sidney, whose infatuation with Essex's sister, Penelope, is recorded in his poem 'Astrophel and Stella'. This romantic link was strengthened when one of Essex's followers, the Earl of Rutland, married Sidney's daughter. But the occupants of Essex House (including the Bacon brothers) also had an unsavoury reputation for homosexuality, and it was said that the Earl of Southampton pursued Sidney's younger brother Robert. In addition to these romantic attachments, however, Essex House was an important centre of culture. Sidney's reputation as a poet was reflected in the presence of Edmund Spenser as a guest and in Southampton's patronage of Shakespeare. It was Essex who aroused Francis Bacon's interest in the new 'natural philosophy', and his masterpiece *The*

Right: Statue of Sir Francis Bacon, Gray's Inn.

Below: Table 3. The Earls of Essex and Leicester and Philip Sidney.

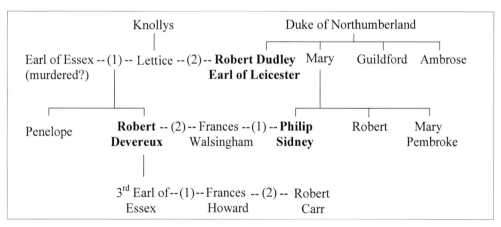

Advancement of Learning was written at the estate in Twickenham which was given to him by the Earl. Science and technology were represented by Dr John Dee and medicine was represented by three of the most notorious physicians of the time, the Doctors Moffett (see page 42), Lopez and Forman.

DR RODERIGO LOPEZ (1525-1594)

Roderigo Lopez was a Marrano, an émigré Portugese Jew. Under Moslem rule, the Jews of the Iberian Peninsula had enjoyed a recognised place in society, but with the expulsion of the

Islamic invaders at the end of the fifteenth century they found themselves classified as heretics in a staunchly Catholic country. Many fled but others, while secretly maintaining the observations of their own faith, 'converted' to Christianity. It was a ruse which had been used before in times of danger, but on this occasion prolonged isolation and intense indoctrination produced a sect whose worship was a strange blend of Judaism, Christianity and mysticism. Known as the Marranos, they formed a well-educated, closely interrelated community which tended to specialise in trade and medicine and had links with England, the Low Countries and throughout the Mediterranean.

Those who remained in Portugal could not hope to escape notice indefinitely and in the late 1550s the Inquisition finally sniffed out the covert Jew, Roderigo Lopez. Fortunate to escape with the confiscation of his goods, but with his career in ruins, he fled the country and arrived in England around 1562. He joined London's small but influential Marrano community and, through the good offices of one of its leaders, Dr Hector Nunez, soon had an appointment at St Bartholomew's Hospital and a Fellowship of the College of Physicians. His services to the hospital were anything but distinguished, but his success elsewhere was remarkable, for within ten years he was physician to Lord Burghley, to the Earl of Essex and to Sir Francis Walsingham. Within twenty, he was caring for the Earl of Leicester and the Queen.

It was not simply as a physician, however, that Lopez served these magnates. England was involved in a complicated and predominantly cold war designed to undermine Spain, one element of which involved supporting Don Antonio, the pretender to the Portugese throne. This process, which was not helped by the duplicity of Don Antonio himself, produced a vast network of agents and double agents involved in conveying and opening mail, espionage, secret negotiations and attempted assassinations. To powerful players who did not wish to become personally involved, Marranos like Lopez, with their knowledge of Continental languages, their secure lines of communication and their bases throughout Europe, were ideal pawns in this game. But Lopez also saw this as a means of advancement and tried, at two levels, to play for both sides. In England, he undertook commissions for Essex and for his rival Burghley. This became evident when Essex, finding that his 'news' was always known at court, realised that it was first being passed to his rival. Nor was his anger assuaged when a drunken Lopez revealed that he had been treating the Earl for a venereal infection. Far worse, however, was the fact that Lopez had of his own accord started secret negotiations with the Spanish government. To the extent that these were in part overtures for peace, his activities, although unofficial, were in line with government policy. The same, however, could not be said of a plot to assassinate a fugitive from the court of Spain who was now a guest at Essex House.

With the capture of various agents and double agents, these matters eventually came to light but the discovery that Lopez had been negotiating with the Spanish did not prove to be the intelligence coup Essex expected. At various times Lopez had been authorised to make such contacts and Burghley, realising that this was as much an attempt to undermine his authority as an attempt to protect security, defended him vigorously. It was only when another prisoner, trying to conceal his involvement in the attempt to assassinate Essex's guest, spoke of a (fictitious) plot to assassinate the Queen that Robert Cecil began to investigate Lopez's contacts more carefully. He soon uncovered a network of intrigue which, if revealed, would have had a devastating effect on his father's position and it quickly became evident that Lopez had to be silenced. As a result, Essex, who by now was also making wild accusations about plots to murder Walsingham and the Queen, found to his amazement that Burghley was anxious to prosecute the man he had so recently defended. After questioning at Essex House and a carefully orchestrated trial, the devious Lopez was found guilty of a crime he did not commit,

Quid dabitis

Proditorum finis funis

Lopez compounding to poyson the Queene.

Lopez plotting to kill
Queen Elizabeth.
(Courtesy of the Royal
College of Physicians)

thus achieving the dubious distinction of being the only Fellow of the College of Physicians
to be hanged, drawn and quartered. It may be that Shakespeare, who as a member of the Essex
House set must have watched these events at close quarters, had Lopez in mind when, six years
later, he wrote *The Merchant of Venice*.

Essex's attempts to gain power were unsuccessful and Elizabeth became increasingly irritated
by his petulant behaviour. Eventually, in 1601, having once more fallen from grace following
the mismanagement of a campaign in Ireland, he and a group of supporters tried to raise the
City. The rebellion was quickly crushed and the Earl was arrested in Essex House, tried and
executed. It was a trial that attracted much adverse comment, for Francis Bacon, who along
with his brother had long been supported and promoted by the Earl, played a leading part in
the prosecution. Nor did Bacon gain by this, for, as he ruefully remarked, 'the Queen hath done
somewhat for me, although not in the proportion I hoped'. But the redoubtable Lettice, mother
of the Earl of Essex, who along with her third husband (who was also executed) had been
implicated in the rebellion, lived on to die thirty-three years later at the age of ninety-four.

THE THIRD EARL, SIMON FORMAN AND THE OVERBURY CASE

In due course, Essex House was inherited by the Essex's son, the third Earl, and another tale of
intrigue, unqualified practitioners and murder began to unfold. During her husband's frequent
absences from court, Essex's wife Frances Howard enjoyed the company of Robert Carr, Earl
of Somerset, a favourite of James I who had replaced Robert Cecil as his secretary. When Essex
returned, his wife claimed that the marital union had not been consummated, and she and Carr
pressed James for an annulment and talked of marriage. This idea was opposed by Sir Thomas
Overbury, Carr's influential adviser, who circulated a poem outlining the behaviour that was
expected of a good wife. Infuriated by this opposition, Carr and Howard arranged for Overbury
to be sent to Russia as an ambassador, knowing that this would remove him from court or, if he
refused the appointment, lead to his imprisonment. In April 1613 he was confined to the Tower
where, five months later, he died suddenly and was hastily buried.

Simon Forman. (Courtesy of the
Royal College of Physicians)

Carr and Howard married but, within two years, rumours of foul play forced James to order
an enquiry into the death. Central to this hearing were two letters supposedly written by
Frances Howard to or about a certain Simon Forman, an unlicensed practitioner who, in an
unusually protracted campaign, had been pursued by the College of Physicians for nearly twenty
years. Having been ridiculed, fined and imprisoned by this 'leude company of infernal goddes',
Forman began to fear for his life and fled to Lambeth, where he sought the protection of one
of his patients, the Archbishop of Canterbury. But the Archbishop, who could have given him a
licence to practice, had been suborned by the College, which eventually refused even to accept
a Cambridge medical qualification as evidence of Forman's competence.

Like many of his contemporaries, Forman dabbled in astrology and divination (although this
only accounted for about 10 per cent of his practice) and it might well be that he had provided
Frances Howard with love potions or predicted the outcome of her affairs. But as he died two
years before Overbury, at a time when Overbury was still active at court, it seems improbable
that he had a hand in his death. Questioned by the tribunal, however, Forman's widow admitted
that a Mrs Taylor, who was directly implicated in the supposed murder, had subsequently asked
for and destroyed a mass of letters from Forman's records. By skilful use of this information it
was thus 'shown' that the Countess (who, as a member of the court, could hardly be charged
with such a crime) had been led astray by the 'witch' Taylor and the 'monster' Forman. Taylor
and three of her associates were executed and Howard and Carr served terms of imprisonment.
Essex went on to become an unsuccessful leader of the Parliamentary forces in the Civil War.

THE END OF ESSEX HOUSE

In 1674 Essex House was bought by the property developer Nicholas Barbon (see page 55) who, on hearing that Charles II intended to present it to a favourite, quickly demolished all but a small section used to house the Cotton library. The rest, along with a squalid lane between Essex House and Arundel House, was converted into 'handsome houses, cookhouses, taverns, vaulting schools and new wharves at the lower end for brewers and wood merchants'. It was to Essex Street that Charles Stuart (Bonnie Prince Charlie) made a five-day secret visit five years after the 1745 rebellion, and it was during this visit that he was said to have been received into the Anglican Church at the nearby St Mary le Strand. The area, and in particular a coffee house known as the Grecian, also became very popular with the gentry, lawyers and certain members of the Royal Society. But although the bust of Essex can still be seen on the Grecian, which has now become an inn called the Devereux, and Barbon's staircase still runs down to the river at the end of Essex Street, only the name of the street recalls the great house that once stood on this site.

Above left: The Devereux. Note the bust of the Earl of Essex above the inn sign.

Above right: Barbon's steps at the end of Essex Street

4

PHARMACEUTICAL PROBLEMS

The College of Physicians had two main functions. It had to license those practising medicine within seven miles of the centre of London, a duty that will be discussed in Chapter Eight, and it had to supervise the apothecaries and the drugs they dispensed. The latter was a difficult task, partly because the apothecaries (who in due course were to become general practitioners) had a tendency to work independently and partly because there were disputes – even within the College – as to what should be dispensed. Closely linked with these issues were a rival to the College Dispensary that was published in Fleet Street and the adventures of Dr Moffett, one of the Earl of Essex's medical attendants.

Professional medical advice in medieval England came from one of two sources: the physicians or the apothecaries. Physicians had undergone a long period of training in a university which (supposedly) gave them an understanding of the workings of the body and therefore of the rationale behind treatment. Apothecaries were trained by apprenticeship to prepare and dispense drugs. Physicians favoured rich, sober attire and conducted much of their work in private. Apothecaries wore the emblems of their guild and worked in noisy, well-advertised shops. Physicians made the diagnosis, decided on a course of treatment and instructed the apothecary accordingly. Apothecaries dispensed whatever had been prescribed. Or, to be more accurate, that was what was supposed to happen.

The problem was that physicians were few in number and very expensive. Indeed, in times of crisis, as during the plague, they tended to disappear altogether, having followed their wealthy patients to safety in the countryside. Consequently, there was an increasing tendency for apothecaries to prescribe as well as to dispense and even to charge for their advice. This, of course, was anathema to the physicians, who used various devices to limit their activities.

Despite the best efforts of the physicians – for it is estimated that in one year one in ten of the City's apothecaries was arraigned before the College – it was evident that the apothecaries were flouting their authority. This was not difficult, for they greatly outnumbered the physicians and were associated with the powerful Guild of Grocers. In 1614, therefore, the physicians (many of whom, as medical attendants to the royal family, had easy access) brought to the notice of James I the fact that they were unable to control these difficult subordinates and that, as a result, the dignity of the College was suffering. The solution suggested was that the apothecaries should be separated from their powerful parent company and established as an independent guild, but one whose charter made it absolutely clear that they were under the control of the physicians. This suggestion was opposed by the grocers, who did not want to lose control of the apothecaries, and by the City, which did not want to see the establishment of a guild which (like the College itself) was outside its control. James, however, agreed that while 'grocers are but merchants, the business of an apothecary is a mystery, wherefore I think it is fitting that they be a corporation of themselves'. But although the charter was granted in 1617, it was not fully recognised by the City until 1630. Two years later, the apothecaries purchased the buildings at Blackfriars that were to become their hall.

Apart from the problem of apothecaries making diagnoses and prescribing, another perennial cause of friction between physicians and apothecaries was a dispute as to exactly how various drugs should be prepared. Under the new charter it was therefore agreed that while physicians would refrain from making up and selling drugs, apothecaries (who for their part would not diagnose or prescribe) would adhere to the formulae in a *London Antidotary* to be drawn up by the College.

Above: The north side of the courtyard of Apothecaries' Hall, showing a row of columns that were once part of the covered way built by Henry VIII. (Courtesy of the Worshipful Society of Apothecaries)

Right: The entrance hall of Apothecaries' Hall, the oldest of the London guild halls. The staircase dates from 1671. (Courtesy of the Worshipful Society of Apothecaries)

The idea of a 'dispensatory' was far from new, having first been mooted in 1585. But although the task of writing it had been divided out among various Fellows, it was soon evident that no progress was being made. The problem was that, in the course of their travels and studies on the Continent, some physicians had encountered the teaching of the *enfant terrible* of medicine, Paracelsus. Paracelsus, who had burned the sacred works of Galen in public, favoured new forms of treatment that were a mixture of chemistry, alchemy and magic. To the staunchly Galenist College this was, of course, anathema. But a substantial minority, including Dr Moffett (of whom more later), felt that these new methods had something to recommend them. The result was deadlock. A new committee appointed in 1594, which included Dr Moffett, was no more successful and it was not until 1616 that real progress was made. By this time, the Huguenot physician Mayerne – also an advocate of the new methods and a major player in the establishment of the Company of Apothecaries – had become involved, and as a physician to the royal household it was he who was given the task of writing the dedication to the King.

The College chose as its publisher a man called John Marriot, who had just set up in business at the Sign of the White Fleur de Luce in St Dunstan's churchyard, Fleet Street and, having registered the book in his name at Stationers' Hall, it was he who acquired the sole rights to sell it on behalf of the College. (It has been suggested that the authorities chose a young and inexperienced printer in what proved to be the misguided belief that he would be easier to control.) This *Pharmacopoeia Londoniensis*, which appeared in 1618, was written in Latin (a language few apothecaries could read) and simply listed the most common and useful preparations. Nothing was said about their function and although the new 'chemical' drugs were mentioned it was explained that they were only auxiliary. In many copies, the one section written in English – a royal edict ordering apothecaries to adhere to the formulae printed – was missing.

The first edition of the *Dispensary* was withdrawn almost immediately, ostensibly because it was full of errors as a result of the printer rushing ahead with publication. In fact it seems almost certain that the real reason was an ongoing dispute between the traditionalists and the supporters of Paracelsus, for the printer was not changed and the revised edition also contained many mistakes. The new version was, however, much longer, listed many more simples and compounds and included some discussion on the uses of the drugs mentioned. Over the following years, Marriot continued to produce 'enlarged and corrected editions' of this book (all of which were in fact essentially unchanged) and his relationship with the College deteriorated markedly. But when, armed with the new Printing Act of 1643 (which passed the task of licensing medical books from the Bishop of London to the College), the authorities decided to intervene they found to their horror that, because the book was already registered at Stationers' Hall in Marriot's name, he was beyond their control.

In 1649 the College therefore adopted the only other course open to it and prepared to issue a second (or third) edition of the *Pharmacopoeia* which, although essentially unchanged, would bring the publication back under its control. But just as the book was about to be released it discovered that a radical bookseller had commissioned the apothecary Nicholas Culpeper to produce a version in English. Culpeper started his training, which he never completed, at Simon White's shop at Temple Bar, Fleet Street. Although he worked 'independently' (of the establishment) he was nevertheless a person of considerable ability. On a purely practical basis his book was a significant contribution, for, in addition to being comprehensible, it listed many more drugs and (for the first time) gave clear instructions as to how they were prepared. But this *Physical Directory* went even further, for it also revealed the secret – hitherto guarded by

The first edition of the *London Pharmacopoeia*. (Courtesy of the Royal College of Physicians)

the physicians – of what the drugs were meant to do. Worse still it made plain (in the year in which the King had been executed) that 'God ... will take tyrants away in his Displeasure', mentioning three groups to whom He might direct His attention: priests, physicians and lawyers. The reaction was savage. Culpeper was accused of dangerous ignorance, greed, drunkenness, lechery, atheism and much else. The College itself remained silent but, in a blistering attack, its chemist announced that 'Culpeper hath made Cul-paper, paper fit to wipe one's breeches withal'. Yet although the author and publisher were hauled before a Parliamentary committee, no punishment seems to have been ordered and the book was an immense success. The College, however, did learn from its mistakes and when, shortly after, the same pair produced a translation of Glisson's thesis *On Rickets*, they discovered that this time both the Latin and the English versions had already been registered at Stationers' Hall.

With the restoration of the monarchy at the end of the Commonwealth, the College hoped that the days in which common tradesmen could insult gentlemen-scholars were over. Again, they were wrong. The political asides may have disappeared from Culpeper's book (which was selling as well as ever), but the correct treatment for every disease was now plainly set out in English for all to read and to order from their apothecary. The battle for control dragged on for another forty years, but the monopoly of the physicians had in effect been broken.

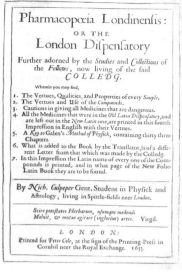

Culpeper's *Physical Directory*. (Courtesy of the Thackray Medical Museum, Leeds)

DR THOMAS MOFFETT (1553-1604)

The intensity of this conflict is well illustrated by the story of Dr Thomas Moffett (who sometimes signed his name Muffet), a man whose varied interests were to bring him into contact with many members of the Essex House clique. Moffett was one of those who had encountered the work of Paracelsus during his travels on the Continent and published an account of these techniques. It was therefore hardly surprising that his application for a Fellowship of the College was rejected. His response, which is reputed to be the rudest letter in the annals of that institution, is addressed to 'such manner of men as I would not vouchsafe to speak unto nor bid them God speed' and ends with the hope that 'God in his justice will confound the College'. But the power of patrons such as the Earl of Essex and Sir Francis Walsingham was not to be ignored and shortly afterwards Moffett, in addition to receiving a Fellowship, achieved the distinction of being made a Censor almost immediately. Perhaps as a sop to the College he then published a much more acceptable commentary on the works of Hippocrates.

Moffett had a close relationship with Walsingham, Elizabeth's 'spymaster' and one of Essex's associates. During his undergraduate years at Cambridge, Moffett had become friendly with a man called Timothy Bright who, apart from being a physician, was renowned as the inventor of 'short, swift, secret writing' (shorthand). This, of course, made Bright useful to Walsingham, who later intervened to obtain an appointment for him at St Bartholomew's Hospital (where he was a disaster) in place of the candidate recommended by the College. But Moffett was also a staunch Protestant with a wide knowledge of the Continent and he too was drawn into Walsingham's circle of spies.

Sadly, this success was short-lived. Walsingham died and the Earl of Essex became involved in a long-running dispute with the College, which was intent on prosecuting another of his medical attendants, Leonard Poe. Moffett had vouched for Poe's competence but his position was undermined when the committee which had drawn up a letter insisting that he should be disciplined met in Moffett's house and was subsequently entertained there. Nor was this the end of his troubles, for his colleague John Dee, 'Elizabeth's magician' (see page 97), had also fallen from favour and his house had been sacked by the mob. Fearing for their safety, many of

Thomas Moffett. (Courtesy of the Royal College of
Physicians)

his fellow practitioners therefore sought sanctuary in Wilton House in Wiltshire. Wilton House
was the home of Mary, Countess of Pembroke (see Table 3), the beautiful, salacious and highly
intelligent sister of Philip Sidney, who was incarcerated there because her much older husband,
the second Earl of Pembroke (who as Henry Herbert had been briefly married to the sister of
Lady Jane Grey), had been warned not to take her to court. Under her influence, the house had
become 'like a little college, there were so many learned and ingenious persons there'. Among
her many interests was Paracelsian chemistry, and one of the 'magicians' who sought refuge
under her roof was the 'godly and learned physician and mathematician Dr Moffett'.

Chemistry, however, was not the only subject that occupied this community. The Countess was
interested in poetry and had worked with various poets, including her illustrious brother. Moffett
also devoted some of his time to writing, producing a biography of Philip Sidney, a book on food
and, most memorably, a book on insects. This had been started by a friend from Cambridge days,
the naturalist Thomas Penny – yet another physician who became a victim of the College when
he practised without a licence in London, and had to be 'rescued' by Walsingham's brother-in-
law. But Penny died before he finished his book on insects and the manuscript was bequeathed
to Moffett, who completed it at Wilton in 1590. On the death of Elizabeth, the dedication was
hastily changed to James I and the book was eventually published by Mayerne. In one of its most
memorable passages it tells of 'a great lady yet living who will not leave off eating spiders', and it has
been suggested that the lady in question was none other than Moffett's new patron, the Countess of
Pembroke. It has also been suggested that it was this poet-Countess who, alluding to Moffett's books
on food and on insects and to his daughter Penelope, retaliated with the nursery rhyme about the
arachnophobic Little Miss Muffet who 'sat on a tuffet, eating her curds and whey'.

5

SOMERSET HOUSE AND SALISBURY COURT

Perhaps the most famous medical event in the history of Fleet Street was the operation to remove a stone from Samuel Pepys' bladder, which took place in a house in the courtyard behind St Bride's. Subsequently, Pepys had many dealings with the medical profession – not least with Graunt and Petty, whose analysis of plague returns was among the first to use mathematical methods in medicine.

For all their splendour, the history of the great Thames-side mansions was one of tragedy as well as triumph. Nowhere was this more evident than in Somerset House, principal home of the Seymours. It was Jane Seymour who eventually presented Henry with Edward, the son he craved, but within days his mother, Henry's most beloved wife, had died. Ten years later Henry himself was dead, and the battle for dynastic and theological control broke out.

There was no doubt that in the first place the throne should go to Edward (1547-1553). But whereas Henry had maintained an essentially Catholic form of worship, the nine-year-old Edward had been trained by Protestant scholars imported from Cambridge by the royal physician Dr Butts (see page 23). To smooth his path, Henry therefore ensured that his court was packed with like-minded men. The Catholic Duke of Norfolk was imprisoned and his loud-mouthed son, the Earl of Surrey, was executed. Gardiner, the conservative Bishop of Winchester, was expressly excluded from the Council and power was vested in the hands of men of proven ability who had the strong support of courtiers, clergy and scholars. In this way, during a potentially dangerous minority, a programme of religious and social reform was implemented and the trimmings of Catholicism were abolished.

The most important member of Edward's Council was Edward Seymour, later Duke of Somerset. Left, as a younger son, to fend for himself at court, his promotion was accelerated by the marriage of his sister Jane to Henry VIII. Aloof, high-handed and politically inept, he tended to ignore his colleagues and incurred much criticism because of his personal gains – which included the great Somerset House. He was, however, an ardent Protestant whose sympathy for the common people earned him the title 'the Good Duke' and was largely responsible for his eventual downfall. By contrast, Edward's other uncle and stepfather, Thomas Seymour, was a man whose great personal charm concealed a conceited, foolish and ambitious nature. Somerset had indeed been warned by his shrewish wife that 'if your brother doesn't die he will

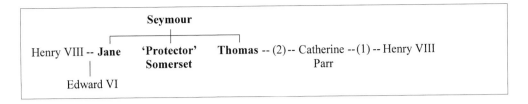

	Seymour		
Henry VIII -- **Jane**	**'Protector'** Somerset	**Thomas** -- (2)-- Catherine --(1) -- Henry VIII Parr	
Edward VI			

Table 4. The Seymours.

be your death'. Having married Henry's widow Catherine Parr, Thomas used his position to become overfamiliar with the young Princess Elizabeth and to ingratiate himself with the boy King. Initially his attempts to undermine his brother's position were successful, but eventually Edward and Elizabeth realised what was happening and distanced themselves. Thomas then used duplicate keys in an attempt to invade the royal bedchamber – a mad escapade during the course of which the King's dog was shot. When the extent of his plotting became evident, his brother ordered his execution. As Elizabeth sapiently observed, 'he was a man of much wit and very little judgement'.

Lurking in the background during these events, which, as he anticipated, further damaged Somerset's standing, was the enigmatic figure of John Dudley, Earl of Warwick and later Duke of Northumberland. Rehabilitated after the execution of his father, Henry VII's unpopular but efficient 'managing director', he too proved to be a man of great ability. Outwardly cold and self-effacing, he was in fact clever, ambitious and ruthlessly efficient. Apparently dedicated to the Protestant cause, he proved to be a talented commander on land and at sea, where he introduced the concept of naval as opposed to 'maritime land' warfare. He employed Thomas Gresham, the son of Richard Gresham (see page 26) to restore the economy. He encouraged exploration and patronised John Dee (see page 97), once a tutor in the Dudley household, who had recently studied with Mercator and other Continental cartographers. And he went to great lengths to ensure that the young Edward was kept fully informed – so much so that he was said to be 'a father to the king, for he governed all'. Sadly his duties brought him into conflict with Somerset and, having once spared his life, he was obliged to order his execution. A few years later, when a foolhardy attempt to preserve the Protestant succession brought about his own downfall, Northumberland confessed that this trial had been engineered and, to the horror of Protestants, re-embraced Catholicism (see page 96).

After the eventful reigns of Mary and Elizabeth, Somerset's great mansion – as yet uncompleted – came into the hands of Anne of Denmark, spendthrift wife of the spendthrift James I, who added a magnificent riverside wing to what became known as Denmark House and, with the aid of Ben Jonson and Inigo Jones, introduced a hedonistic court to a new form of entertainment, the masque. But this revelry was interrupted by the death of Anne's oldest son Prince Henry, a sturdy, sensible individual after whom Prince Henry's Room in the Strand is named. It was even hinted that he might have been poisoned, but the notes of the Royal Physician Mayerne – who was implicated – show that he probably died of typhoid. Be that as it may, it meant that the throne passed to his insecure and pedantic brother, Charles I, with disastrous results. (For the later history of Somerset House, see pages 72 and 108.)

During the Civil War, London became a Parliamentary stronghold. The once Royalist College of Physicians modified its behaviour, arms were stored in Apothecaries' Hall and most of the great Thames-side mansions were taken over by the Army. In the region of St Bride's, the noble Sackvilles of Salisbury House were replaced by the foundling Colonel Pride and the leather-

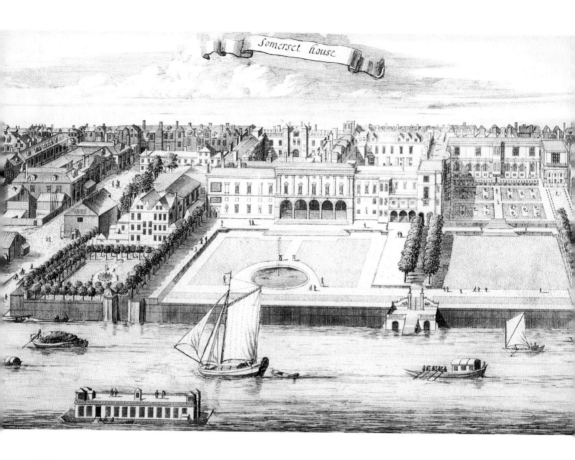

Above: Denmark (Somerset) House. (Courtesy of the Guildhall Library, London)

Left: Prince Henry's Room.

Opposite page: Salisbury Court. (Courtesy of the Guildhall Library, London)

seller Praise-God Barebones; the pulpit of St Bride's was occupied by 'Nonconformist intruders'; and Milton, another Parliamentarian, worked in a house in St Bride's churchyard. But, like all ill winds, these changes had their advantages, for in Salisbury Court – an area that was to be associated with many famous individuals – a certain John Pepys, a 'foreign' (i.e. Cambridgeshire) tailor, was being harassed by the powerful Guild of Merchant Tailors. It was soon brought home to these arrogant Presbyterian merchants that 'levelling' applied to them as well as to Royalist squires, and before long John himself was a member of that august body. Possibly this had something to do with his neighbour in Salisbury Court, the well-respected republican Town Clerk John Sadler. It certainly seems to be more than a coincidence that, two weeks after Sadler was rewarded with the Mastership of Magdalene College, Cambridge, John's son Samuel was admitted as a Sizar of that college.

SAMUEL PEPYS (1632-1703)

Samuel Pepys was born in a house that once stood on the east side of the upper end of Salisbury Court behind St Bride's. In his eventful lifetime he was destined to see the execution of Charles I, to be aboard the ship that brought Charles II back to England and to serve James II until the time of his departure. Before that, however, he was to undergo an ordeal that made him Fleet Street's most illustrious patient, for during the bitter winter of 1657/8 he developed excruciating pains caused by a stone in the bladder. It so happened that one of his neighbours in Salisbury

Court was Thomas Hollier, a well-known lithotomist from the hospitals of St Thomas and St Bartholomew and the man who was shortly to sell the Warwick Lane site to the College of Physicians. It was therefore to Hollier that Pepys turned for help, and on 26 March 1658 he was 'cut for the stone'. Because his own home was small, the operation was done in a larger house in Salisbury Court which belonged to a cousin, and the prescription for the pre-medication, written by Dr Moleyns of St Bartholomew's Hospital (whose grave is in St Bride's) has survived. The procedure, carried out in the presence of his family, was a success (unlike four subsequent operations done by the same surgeon) and thereafter on the anniversary of the operation Pepys

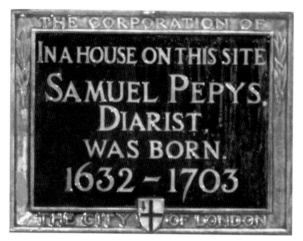

THE CORPORATION OF

IN A HOUSE ON THIS SITE
SAMUEL PEPYS,
DIARIST,
WAS BORN.
1632 ~ 1703

THE CITY OF LONDON

Left: Pepys' birthplace, Salisbury Court.

Below: 'Cutting for the stone'. (Courtesy of the Thackray Medical Museum, Leeds)

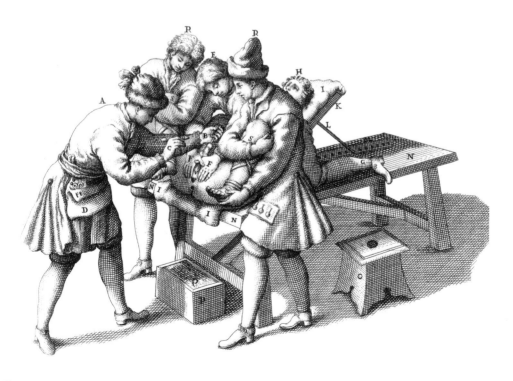

held 'a solemn feast for the cutting of the stone', an object the size of a tennis ball which he was always happy to produce for inspection. He also continued to consult Hollier – for example about 'a decay in my memory' when he most uncharacteristically forgot an appointment to show the (disguised) wife of a colleague over the fleet while her husband was out of town. He was advised to cut down on his drinking!

Having surmounted this hazard and contrived, by a combination of diligence and good fortune, to retain his post at the Admiralty during the Restoration, Pepys went from strength to strength. Thirteen years after his father begged the mighty Guild of Merchant Tailors to fund his university education, he was back in Salisbury Court in a coach-and-six (admittedly borrowed) for the funeral of a relative. He received the Freedom of the City for his services as a governor of Christ's Hospital and was treated by one of its young physicians, Dr Hans Sloane, a fellow bibliophile to whom he wrote 'I almost wish myself sick that I might have the pretence to invite you for an hour or two to another visit by yourself'. (Later in life he was also attended by John Radcliffe whose house was in Bow Street near Covent Garden.) While at Christ's he established a cadre of mathematicians (for whom Hooke designed a special badge) to produce navigators for the Royal Navy. He was a governor of the Bridewell and was mortified, during a period of unpopularity, to discover a pamphlet alluding to his amorous activities and asking that anyone who knew his whereabouts should inform the head of that institution. He was a governor of St Thomas's Hospital and became president of the Royal Society, which Evelyn asked him to attend at a time when it was in danger of dissolution, and his imprimatur is to be found on the title page of Newton's *Principia*. (For an account of Pepys' later homes, see page 61).

Pepys had many contacts with members of the medical profession. He attended dissections, watched (unsuccessful) attempts to transfuse a dog at the Royal Society and heard lectures in the theatre of Barber Surgeons' Hall. At one of these lectures he saw and admired Holbein's painting of Henry VIII bestowing the royal charter, and three years later (following the Great Fire) he returned with the intention of buying it. This purchase did not take place because, when he saw it for a second time, he deemed it 'a pleasant but not a good picture, so spoiled that I have no mind to it'. Perhaps more significantly he also found that the asking price (£1,000) was five times that which he had in mind. But his most curious contact with the profession occurred in 1682 when the flagship taking the Duke of York to Edinburgh ran aground and sank. Among the survivors picked up by the escort on which Pepys was sailing was the physician Sir Charles Scarburgh, 'almost dead after long exposure to cold water and an Homeric struggle for a plank with the Duke's dog Mumper'. (In the face of this disaster the Duke is said to have ordered 'Save the dogs and Col. Churchill'). His main contact, however, was with 'that volcano of learned ingenuity' Sir William Petty. Pepys, who called him 'my Irish Apollo', held him in high regard but the Secretary to the Navy was not alone in being irritated by Petty's obsession with naval architecture and in particular with his unsatisfactory designs for a 'double-bottomed boat' (i.e. a catamaran). This vessel, which was ridiculed by the King and which capsized, killing the crew, on its maiden voyage, eventually forced the exasperated Pepys to 'solicit Sir William Petty to make an end of his scheme of naval philosophy and to consider the old saying among the divines "Qui nescit orare discat navigare" [Those who don't know how to pray should learn to sail]'.

PLAGUE

There was, however, at least one major medical problem that Petty must have discussed with Pepys. In June 1665, while waiting anxiously for news of a naval battle at Lowestoft, Pepys noticed 'three red crosses on doors in Drury Lane'. Within days, London was in the grip of the plague and the number of funerals at St Bride's rose steadily from less than 10 to as many as 238 in a week. During the worst of this period the bearers were living in the church and, as Pepys observed, even during the long winter nights it was not possible to inter all the bodies during the hours of darkness. In all, the parish lost 2,111 of its members, including two churchwardens, and it was not until May 1666 that the vicar was able to record 'no one death this week'. Overall, a sixth of the population, 80,000 people, died – the equivalent of the populations of the next five largest cities in the country.

It was, of course, a problem that London had faced for many years. Major outbreaks of plague had occurred in 1563, 1593, 1603, 1625 and 1640, and the outbreak of 1603 (which again killed one in five of the population) prevented all ceremonies at the time of James I's arrival in London. Henry Holland, vicar of St Bride's, had written on *Spiritual Preservations Against the Pestilence*, but in dedicating his book to the mayor, aldermen and sheriffs was no doubt hoping that the more earthly problem of cleaning out the Fleet Ditch would be taken in hand. Towards the end of the sixteenth century, efforts were made to record the incidence and to limit the spread of the disease. 'Searchers' were appointed to identify it and, when it occurred, 'watchers' were supposed to mark the house with a cross and confine the other occupants. But the searchers were often old people who could do no other work, and they and the watchers were frequently bribed to 'overlook' this fateful condition. The information they passed on to parish clerks was therefore far from accurate. Nevertheless it was from this information that the Company of Parish Clerks compiled the so-called 'Bills of Mortality'.

1665.

A TABLE of the
CHRISTENINGS and MORTALITY

For the Year 1664 and 1665. *

Weeks.	Days of the Month.	Chrift.	Bur.	Pla.	Par. infec.	Weeks.	Days of the Month.	Chrift.	Bur.	Pla.	Par. infec.
1	Dec. 27.	229	291	1	1	27	June 27.	199	684	267	20
2	January 3.	239	349	0	0	28	July 4.	207	1006	470	33
3	10.	235	394	0	0	29	11.	197	1268	725	40
4	17.	223	415	0	0	30	18.	194	1761	1089	54
5	24.	237	474	0	0	31	25.	193	2785	1843	68
6	31.	216	409	0	0	32	Auguft 1.	215	3014	2010	73
7	Febr. 7.	221	393	0	0	33	8.	178	4030	2817	86
8	14.	224	462	1	1	34	15.	166	5319	3880	96
9	21.	232	393	0	0	35	22.	171	5568	4237	103
10	28.	233	396	0	0	36	29.	169	7496	6102	113
11	March 7.	236	441	0	0	37	Septem. 5.	167	8252	6988	118
12	14.	236	433	0	0	38	12.	168	7690	6544	119
13	21.	221	363	0	0	39	19.	176	8297	7165	126
14	28.	238	353	0	0	40	26.	146	6460	5533	123
15	April 4.	242	344	0	0	41	October 3.	142	5720	4929	124
16	11.	245	382	0	0	42	10.	141	5068	4327	126
17	18.	237	344	0	0	43	17.	147	3219	2665	114
18	25.	229	398	2.	1	44	24.	104	1806	1421	104
19	May 2.	237	388	0	0	45	31.	104	1388	1031	97
20	9.	211	347	9	4	46	Novem. 7.	95	1787	1414	110
21	16.	227	353	3	2	47	14.	113	1359	1050	99
22	23.	231	385	14	3	48	21.	108	905	652	84
23	30.	229	400	17	5	49	28.	112	544	333	60
24	June 6.	234	405	43	7	50	Decem. 5.	123	428	210	48
25	13.	206	558	112	12	51	12.	133	442	243	57
26	20.	204	615	168	19	52	19.	147	525	281	68

The Totals { Chriftened — — 9967
Buried — — 97306
Whereof of the Plague 68596

* Bell's London's Remembrancer.

A General

Left: Bills of Mortality. (Courtesy of the Thackray Medical Museum, Leeds)

These Bills of Mortality attracted the attention of a haberdasher called John Graunt (1620-74), who is buried in St Dunstan's in the West, Fleet Street (better known for its association with another Fleet Street clothier, the fisherman Izaak Walton). Graunt had an interest in mathematics and, in one of the earliest examples of the use of statistical methods in medicine, employed this technique to study the figures and produce a paper entitled *Natural and Political Observations Mentioned in a Following Index and Made upon the Bills of Mortality* (1662). This work greatly impressed Anthony Wood, who described Graunt as 'the most ingenious person [considering his education and employment] that his time hath produced, learning like this being very rare in a trader or mechanic'. It also came to the notice of Charles II who, demonstrating that egalitarianism which the College of Physicians so disliked in the Royal Society, recommended Graunt as one of its original members and told the president that 'if you find any more such tradesmen they should be admitted without more ado'. But despite his occupation Graunt was clearly not without influence, for he helped Petty to obtain the Chair of Music at Gresham College – an interesting sideline for the Reader in Anatomy at the University of Oxford. For his part, Petty, who was himself a mathematician, took a great interest in Graunt's work (which he called political arithmetic), editing the fifth edition and coming to speak of it as if it was his own. So in 1687, anxious to get royal sanction for the publication of his studies on statistics and political economy, we find the now Sir William Petty writing to Pepys: 'I thank God that his Majesty appointed you to examine these my opinions'.

6

DESTRUCTION

The Great Fire, Nicholas Barbon and York House

The City, including the majority of Fleet Street, was destroyed by the Great Fire. But further west another form of destruction was taking place as Nicholas Barbon, doctor turned property developer, demolished some of the great mansions. Chief among these was York House, birthplace of two famous collections and home of the Bacons and of a murdered courtier who may himself have been a murderer.

Although less costly in terms of life, for it is said only to have killed eight people, the Great Fire which followed the plague was a disaster that caused unimaginable destruction. Starting near old London Bridge, it was swept westwards by the prevailing wind, feeding on the closely packed, timber-built, pitch-clad houses and on stores of oil, tallow and spirits in riverside warehouses. London Bridge itself was spared because an earlier conflagration had destroyed several of the houses on it, creating a firebreak. But the only house rebuilt at the north end collapsed, blocking this line of escape and destroying the wheel that pumped water to the city. With only a rudimentary water supply and a few rickety handpumps (there is no record that the one at St Bride's was even used), it seemed indeed that there was nothing the citizens could do to control the blaze. It was Pepys who, practical as ever, raced up the Thames to Whitehall and dragged the King and the Duke of York out of a service to take charge of the situation. Both responded personally, the Duke nearly losing his life when, with molten lead from the roof of St Paul's pouring down Ludgate Hill, he and his troops tried to blast a firebreak across the end of Fleet Street. But the flames outflanked them, leaping the Fleet and destroying the Bridewell, Salisbury Court and St Bride's as they moved relentlessly westwards. In the east, where the spread of the fire was slowed by the prevailing wind, Pepys summoned workers from the dockyard to save the Navy Office. To the north, Gresham College (near the site of the NatWest Tower) had a narrow escape, and a party led by Evelyn contrived to save Staple Inn on Holborn. But in the west, where Charles had 'refreshed' those creating firebreaks with handfuls of coins, preparations were being made to demolish Somerset House and much of the Strand when a timely fall in the wind finally halted the destruction just short of Prince Henry's Room near Temple Bar.

It is almost impossible to convey the extent of this disaster. The City had virtually ceased to exist and the damage, far greater than that seen in the Blitz, was magnified by the fact that surrounding areas were unscathed. After passing the lawns and trees of Whitehall, the Thames-side mansions in the Strand and a double line of houses at Temple Bar, those approaching from the west were suddenly confronted with a scene of utter desolation that stretched as far

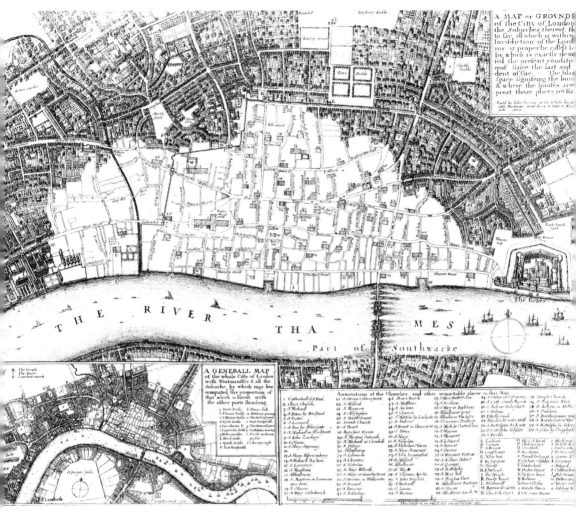

Hollar's map of the Great Fire. Gresham College is the small square courtyard marked T (in the north-east corner, just outside the area of destruction). (Courtesy of the Guildhall Library, London)

as the eye could see. This transition is perhaps best illustrated by looking at an enlargement of the south-west corner of Hollar's map of the stricken city. Moving from the west, the elegant gardens of Essex House, Middle Temple Hall, the round Temple church, Temple Bar, St Dunstan's and the houses in Chancery Lane are untouched. But beyond that the paper is blank, indicating that everything has been destroyed. (A plaque on the Templars' buttery in Elm Tree Court in the Temple records the destruction of Fig Tree Court in 1666.) It was the same in the east, where, beyond the crowded streets of Tower Hill and the trees round the Navy Office, only the rickety towers of ruined churches protruded from a sea of rubble 4ft deep. St Paul's, the Guildhall, the Exchange, 87 churches, 13,000 houses and the halls of 44 guilds (many of them converted medieval mansions) had been destroyed. Christ's Hospital, the Bridewell, the College of Physicians, Apothecaries' Hall and much of Barber Surgeons' Hall had gone and 100,000 people had been rendered homeless. Nor was the disaster purely physical, for London, the third largest city in the world, was the commercial capital of the country. Recently ravaged by plague

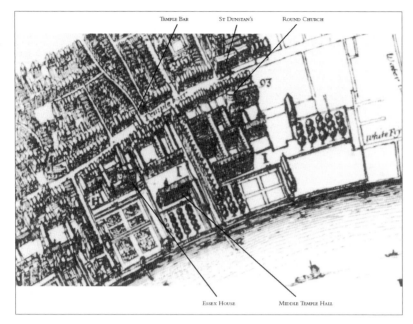

TEMPLE BAR   ST DUNSTAN'S   ROUND CHURCH

ESSEX HOUSE   MIDDLE TEMPLE HALL

An enlargement of the south-west corner of the 'fire' map, showing how Essex House, Middle Temple Hall, Temple church, Temple Bar, St Dunstan's in the West and Chancery Lane survived unscathed.

and impoverished by war, it was preparing, in the midst of a naval conflict, to lay up a fleet it could no longer afford. Now, for the moment, its one source of revenue was a tax on the import after which Seacoal Lane, north of Fleet Street, is named.

Restoration was a matter of urgency. The Bridewell was rebuilt in 1667 and at Blackfriars, where some of the old walls had survived, reconstruction of Apothecaries' Hall to the original design was started in 1668. This produced a building which, having survived an unexploded bomb in the Blitz, was to become the oldest Company Hall in the City. Rubble from the ruins of St Paul's was used to level Fleet Street (the first street to be surveyed and rebuilt) and the Fleet itself was cleaned out and provided with new wharfs and bridges – an exercise which, in the opinion of one critic, 'would only harbour toads, frogs and other vermin and benefit a few peddling coal-merchants'. By 1671 the churchwardens of St Bride's were entertaining Wren and Hooke at the Globe tavern in Fleet Street (at a cost of £2 17s) and this, with a further 6s 6d 'spent at Mr Hodersall's giving the Doctor Wren a treate', ensured that their church (as yet without its distinctive spire) was one of the first and most expensive to be reopened. So, from the surrounding desolation, new buildings gradually emerged to link up with the area in and beyond the Temple that had survived.

But as one part of London was being rebuilt, another was about to be destroyed. Under the Tudors, building in the suburbs had been strictly regulated 'lest it fill upp that small Remaynder of Ayre'. James I had adopted a more liberal policy, provided that the new property was built of brick, but this objective was not realised and by 1630 there were complaints that the Strand, once a pleasant and exclusive suburb, was being invaded by fish-stalls, sheds and newly erected tenements. There were admittedly developments 'fitt for the habitacions of Gentlemen and men of ability', like the Covent Garden estate erected by the Earl of Bedford which even had a water supply to each house, but the fact remained that the aristocrats living along the bank of the Thames were being hemmed in by the 'lower orders'. There were, moreover, newer and more attractive houses in the region of St James's Palace, and it was to these that the owners of the Thames-side mansions now began to move.

Right: The Fig Tree Court plaque, Temple.

Below: The mouth of the Fleet after restoration, showing St Bride's, the Bridewell and the remains of the colonnade from Blackfriars. (Courtesy of the Guildhall Library, London)

NICHOLAS BARBON (1640-1698)

This provided yet another opportunity for the property developers, and in particular for a certain Dr Nicholas Barbon. Nicholas was the son of Praise-God Barebones, the Baptist leather-seller from Fleet Street who gave his name to one of Cromwell's parliaments. He was indeed rather good at giving names, for he had named his son 'If Jesus had not died for thy sins thou hadst been damned'. Barbon was not only an MD of Leyden but also – surprisingly for a Nonconformist – an honorary Fellow of the College. Indeed he was probably among the seventy-three honorary Fellows created in 1664 whose subscriptions were stolen the following year when the curator deserted the College during the plague. But he also had other, more lucrative interests. He was

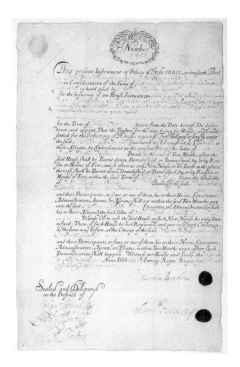

Above left: A fire insurance policy signed by Barbon. (Courtesy of the Museum of London)

Above right: No. 1 New Court, Temple, by Barbon.

something of an economist and has indeed been quoted by Marx, although Macaulay clearly regarded him as a crook: 'One of those shrewd men who is perfectly willing to be authorised by law to pay £100 with £80'. In the aftermath of 1666, he entered the profitable occupation of fire insurance, and in due course his business behind the Royal Exchange became the Phoenix. But above all, to use Porter's memorable phrase, he was the 'Adam of speculative builders'. His projects were characterised by two things – they were large and they were lucrative. They weren't necessarily legal, however, for if the existing owners (who would be kept waiting in his palatial home in Crane Court off Fleet Street) did not respond to his requests, bribes or threats he simply ignored them and went ahead with his work regardless. This of course tended to cause difficulties. Sometimes, as when the benchers of Gray's Inn objected to his development at Red Lion Square and drove his workmen out, there was violence. But Barbon returned the next day with an army of 200 and made it clear that no matter how many 'troops' were required, they would be produced. The building proceeded. More often he appeared in court, but here he contrived to outwit his opponents with an outward appearance of charm and understanding and a masterly array of delaying tactics. Utterly unscrupulous and dishonest, he was nevertheless something of a genius.

So it was, in the aftermath of the Great Fire, that Barbon built new homes for the residents of the overcrowded and now derelict city. Some, like No.1 New Court in the Temple, were magnificent. Some were frankly dangerous. But the majority favoured a simple, repetitive style that was cheap to produce and yet had a veneer of gentility – jerry-building, as one commentator has it, which is now protected by preservation orders. The developments on the site of York House are typical of his work.

Among an unprepossessing collection of streets on the east side of Charing Cross station there is a small thoroughfare called 'York Place – formerly Of Alley'. Along with the nearby George Street, Villiers Street, Duke Street and Buckingham Street, it is a reminder that this was once the site of York House, home of George Villiers, Duke of Buckingham (1592-1628), of which only one fragment remains. The first mansion on this site, Norwich House, was built for the Bishops of Norwich early in the thirteenth century. Confiscated by Henry VIII, it was subsequently given by Mary to the Archbishop of York. Within two years, however, in 1558, it had become the home of Nicholas Bacon, Lord Keeper of the Great Seal. His son Francis Bacon was born here in 1561 and it was here that the first trial of his patron, the Earl of Essex, which he masterminded, was held (see page 35). In 1617 Francis himself became Lord Keeper, but within four years he was dismissed in disgrace – partly for taking bribes and partly because, as Aubrey records, he was a 'paiderostos'. A pamphlet thrown into the grounds of York House made play on his name, saying:

> Within this sty a hog doth lie
> Who must be hanged for sodomy.

Bacon retired to the estate at Twickenham, which he had been given by the Earl, hoping that his new patron, the Duke of Buckingham, would ease his return to favour. In fact Villiers had designs on York House, which the bankrupt Bacon was eventually obliged to sell to him.

Villiers' occupation of York House is associated with two great collections and one, or possibly two, murders. At this time, the development of overseas possessions had made the collection of 'curiosities' a popular recreation in polite society. This hobby, which began with the acquisition of exotic plants and trees for the gardens of the aristocracy, had developed into the wholesale collection of animals, minerals and objects of interest of all sorts. London had two famous collections of this kind, one started by Sir Hans Sloane and the other started by a certain John Tradescant. Tradescant, the Duke of Buckingham's gardener, who conducted many of his expeditions in person, had a reputation for designing gardens full of exotic trees and plants. Encouraged by his employer, however, he expanded his interest to incorporate all manner of curiosities, and after Buckingham's death his collection (now housed in Lambeth) became one of

Of Alley.

Visscher's panorama of 1616, showing Whitehall, York House, Durham House and Bedford House.

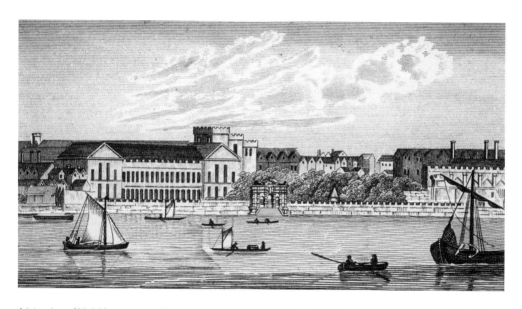

A later view of York House, now with a watergate, and Durham House. (Courtesy of the Guildhall Library, London)

the sights of London. When he himself died in 1638, his son, John Tradescant junior, enlisted the aid of the physician Thomas Wharton and the lawyer Elias Ashmole to catalogue the collection. Ashmole, whose personal collection of coins and medals had been destroyed in the Temple fire of 1679, was ingenious enough to obtain a written agreement that, when Tradescant and his wife died, he was to inherit the collection. Realising their error, both Tradescant and his widow subsequently tried to revoke the agreement, but without success. Ashmole moved into the house next door and there followed a series of events that reflected badly on both parties. Ashmole constructed an illicit means of access and removed choice items from a collection which he had not yet inherited. Mrs Tradescant, on the other hand, sold exhibits in defiance of the agreement and eventually, possibly as a result of the harassment to which she was subjected, was found drowned in a pond in the garden of her home. Unabashed by this disaster, Ashmole announced that 'Because the knowledge of Nature is very necessary to humaine life and health ... and useful in Medicine' he would bestow the 'great variety of natural Concretes and Bodies which I have amass'd' on the University of Oxford to form the basis of its museum. It is ironic that Tradescant's plants, the first component of his collection, were forgotten, for Oxford already had a botanical garden.

The origins of the second collection were more complex. It had been suggested that James I's surviving son, Prince Charles, should marry the Infanta of Spain. Despite the unpopularity of this idea and the Continental wars which made such an event highly improbable, Villiers, a royal favourite, and Charles obtained permission to go incognito to view the prospective bride. (Described as 'a most entrancingly beautiful boy', Villiers had been introduced to James by George Abbott, one of the translators of the King James Bible and later Archbishop of Canterbury, in the hope that personal benefit would flow from the connection; it did not.) Using assumed names, and wearing false whiskers that soon fell off, the pair departed for Spain in the company of Matthew Wren, uncle of the great architect. They were, of course, discovered and the Spanish, barely able to believe that they had obtained two such valuable hostages, imposed conditions that were utterly unacceptable. The marriage never took place but, as a result of his visit to Madrid, Charles developed a passion for art which, in a Continent torn apart by war, he was well able to develop. His collection, which was on view in the Stone Gallery of Whitehall, was broken up during the Civil War. The Spanish Ambassador contrived to get many of the finest items but other treasures were handed out in lieu of cash to the most improbable owners, who hastily sold them off 'at very reasonable prices'. In later years, Charles II (who had tuition from the artist Hollar, then living at Arundel House) was to make considerable efforts to reassemble this great collection made by his father.

Despite being the King's favourite, and possibly his lover, Buckingham was well aware that he was deeply unpopular. There was of course jealousy about the fact that the son of a servant woman should have attained a rank normally reserved for those of royal blood. More importantly, however, it was suspected that Villiers – who was thought to have Catholic sympathies – had occasioned the death of James I during what seemed at first to be a fairly minor illness. Anxious to improve his standing, he therefore planned a raid to relieve the Huguenots of La Rochelle, but before this took place he was stabbed to death by a naval lieutenant from Fleet Street called John Felton. Although this was partly due to anger at his own lack of promotion and the success of those who had never seen active service, Felton seems also to have shared Parliament's resentment of Buckingham's corrupt and luxurious lifestyle. He was imprisoned in the Bridewell, where there were extensive records of prisoners being tortured, but for some obscure reason an assembly of judges agreed that 'by the law of the land he might not be tortured on the rack, for no such punishment is known or allowed by our law'. Buckingham's daughter, Lady Mary Villiers, was virtually adopted by Charles I and recently, when her portrait by Van Dyck was restored, Charles' cipher was found on the back, showing that it was once part of the royal collection.

During the Civil War, York House was used by Fairfax but in 1657, when John Sheffield, the second Duke of Buckingham (who was a strong supporter of the Society of Chemical Physicians (see page 66) and had a laboratory at York House) married Fairfax's daughter, it once more

Above left: Buckingham Street looking south, showing the York Watergate, the Hungerford Suspension Bridge and (on the right) Barbon's York Buildings. (Courtesy of the Museum of London)

Above right: The York Watergate, the only surviving relic of York House. (Courtesy of the Guildhall Gallery London and the family of William Alister MacDonald)

York Buildings. The house on the right, No. 12, which was built by Barbon, was used by Pepys. No. 14, in which he also lived, was subsequently demolished and rebuilt.

became the property of his family. In fact it was rarely used and in 1670 Barbon, along with two other speculators (one of whom was Pepys' disciple Anthony Deane) bought the site and demolished the entire building, with the exception of Inigo Jones' watergate, which still stands in Embankment Gardens.

One part of the resulting development, No. 12 Buckingham Street, is of particular interest. This house was leased by Will Hewer, a protégé of Pepys and Chief Clerk to the Admiralty. When Pepys was out of favour and out of office, Hewer gave him a home at this address and later, when Pepys imported his mistress, Hewer himself moved out. In 1684 the building was nearly lost when fire broke out two doors away in No. 14, destroying a dozen houses in York Buildings. Pepys' house was saved by the timely arrival of the Guards, who blew up No. 13, thus preserving No. 12 and its fine seventeenth-century staircase. But a few years later, when No. 14 (which stands on the riverside just behind the York Watergate) had been rebuilt, Pepys took over this address and got permission to use it as the Admiralty Office. (During part of his visit to England in 1698 Peter the Great lodged in No. 15 on the opposite side of the street. As one of the main purposes of his visit was to study shipbuilding, it seems to be a remarkable coincidence that he should chose to live so near to the greatest authority on the British Navy. There appears however to be no record of a meeting between the two – the diary, of course, had ended thirty years earlier. Pepys' second house, No. 14, was rebuilt for a second time in 1791.) Pepys' library was installed here and he had the Lord High Admiral's crown and anchor engraved on the river frontage. The real ownership of the house was indeed forgotten and when, after the departure of James II, Pepys resigned, he had to resist a claim that the building was Crown property.

The effect of this development on the Thames waterfront can best be appreciated by comparing the array of elegant mansions shown on page 58 with the jumble of housing shown on page 62, drawn in 1749. But for builders such as Barbon it was an era of great prosperity, and at one time he was even able to buy the great Tudor mansion at Osterley belonging to the Lord Mayor, Sir Thomas Gresham. Eventually, however, this rather unsavoury entrepreneur overreached himself and was declared bankrupt, although his name is still commemorated in Barbon Close opposite Great Ormond Street.

Pepys' library in No. 14 Buckingham Street. (Courtesy of the Guildhall Library, London)

SOMERSET HOUSE ST MARY LE STRAND SITE OF ARUNDEL HOUSE MIDDLE TEMPLE HALL TEMPLE CHURCH WHITEFRIARS ST BRIDES
ESSEX HOUSE (ALSATIA) BRIDEWELL

WATERTOWER SITE OF DURHAM HOUSE RUINED SAVOY SOMERSET HOUSE
ST MARTINS
YORK BUILDING
YORK WATERGATE

Above: The Bucks' panorama of the Thames bank, 1749. Apart from the York Watergate, the ruins of the Savoy, Somerset House and the Temple, all the original buildings have been demolished. (Courtesy of the Guildhall Library, London)

A Barbon memorial off Great Ormond Street. (Courtesy of the Guildhall Library, London)

7

THE TEMPLE, THE ROYAL SOCIETY AND ARUNDEL HOUSE

The Seymour family had an unhappy history. Jane, the one wife Henry mourned, died soon after producing his longed-for son and heir. Thomas, who rebuilt Arundel House and married Henry's widow Catherine Parr, was executed for overfamiliarity with the stepdaughter who was to become Queen Elizabeth. Edward's guardian, 'Protector' Somerset, suffered the same fate before his great mansion was completed. And of the subsequent owners of Arundel House, one died in the Tower, one died in exile and one died in poverty. But the two great houses with which the Seymours were associated, Arundel House and Somerset House, played an important part in the history of the Royal Society, which extended the tradition of learning in Fleet Street that was started by the Church and the Temple.

In 1162 a religious order of knights moved from Holborn to Fleet Street on the western boundary of the City. Founded in 1118 to protect pilgrims to the Holy Land, its members, known as Templars because their base in Jerusalem was on the site of Solomon's Temple, were dedicated to a life of chastity and austerity. They built a magnificent monastery with a 'hall of priests' and a 'hall of knights', erected posts and a chain outside their new home to mark the boundary of the City (Temple Bar) and, in 1185, dedicated the famous church (in which Dr Richard Mead is buried). Like their churches elsewhere, it was round, supposedly in imitation of the Dome of the Rock. Among the many establishments on this section of Thames bank, the Temple is the only one that has survived for 800 years. It was not, however, to remain in the hands of the Templars, for by degrees they had became more powerful, wealthy and secretive and in 1307, amid charges of immorality, the order was dissolved by the Pope. Their land then passed into the hands of the Knights Hospitallers of St John, who leased all but the ecclesiastical buildings and the Outer Temple (Essex Street) to the lawyers.

Until the beginning of the thirteenth.century, lawyers had met their clients in St Paul's and there was a school of law in the precincts of the cathedral. But when Henry III, anxious to promote his new foundations at Oxford, banned the teaching of law within the City, the lawyers moved to accommodation outside the City walls provided by the Bishop of Lincoln (Lincoln's Inn), Lord Gray de Wilton (Gray's Inn) and the Temple. The Temple was confiscated by the Crown during the Reformation, but the freehold was presented to the Benchers by James I in 1608 and in 1732 the Middle and Inner Temples separated to form the last of the four Inns of Court.

Temple church.

The Inns of Court, now the preserve of the barristers, are independent, virtually self-governing organisations, each presided over by a Master and Benchers, which alone have the power to call students to the Bar. Probably founded in the fourteenth century, their original purpose was to teach, control and protect those studying law. The course of instruction, which lasted seven years, was broad and included subjects such as history, singing and dancing, and students, like those at the two universities, were required to wear gowns, to 'keep' terms, to attend hall and chapel – and to have their beards trimmed every three weeks. Even in appearance the Inns of Court were (and are) very like the colleges of Oxford and Cambridge and their quiet, virtually unknown gardens have changed little since Boswell wrote that:

the Temple is a most agreeable place. You quit all the hurry and bustle of the City in Fleet Street and the Strand, and all at once find yourself in a pleasant academic retreat. You see good convenient buildings and handsome walks, you view the silver Thames and you are shaded by venerable trees.

It was from the garden of the Middle Temple that the red and white roses that became the emblems of the Wars of the Roses were supposedly plucked.

Activity in the Inns of Court reached a peak between 1550 and 1650, when there were about 1,000 lawyers and law students in the area. Indeed, it became customary for many young men to spend two years in one of the Inns 'to see a little life and to learn a little law'. It was an agreeable milieu, for the presence of the legal fraternity promoted luxury trades and gave the area a reputation for brightness and elegance. The Middle Temple Hall, whose magnificent double hammer-beam roof dates from 1573, was always the scene of lavish masques, plays, banquets and revels between All Saint's Day (1 November) and Candlemas (2 February). Nevertheless, by the latter part of the seventeenth century legal education began to decline and by the end of the eighteenth it had virtually ceased. Thereafter there was a strong recovery and the chambers of barristers now extend well beyond the confines of the Inns.

THE ROYAL SOCIETY

Towards the end of the seventeenth century, a second group of scholars made its appearance. For some time there had been a growing feeling that, if scientific progress was to be made, the traditional teaching of men such as Galen and Aristotle would have to be abandoned and the 'charming amusement of forming hypotheses replaced by the toilsome drudgery of making observations'. But Bacon, who championed this view, realised that 'it was idle to expect any great advance from grafting new things onto old'. Instead, existing methods would have to be completely replaced with a painstaking, co-ordinated programme of authenticated experiments. This, of course, was the approach adopted by Harvey, who first presented his work on the circulation to an unresponsive College in 1616. But it was the Parliamentary 'purge' of 1648 that brought to Oxford a group from Gresham College who were already thinking along these lines and were to establish the movement.

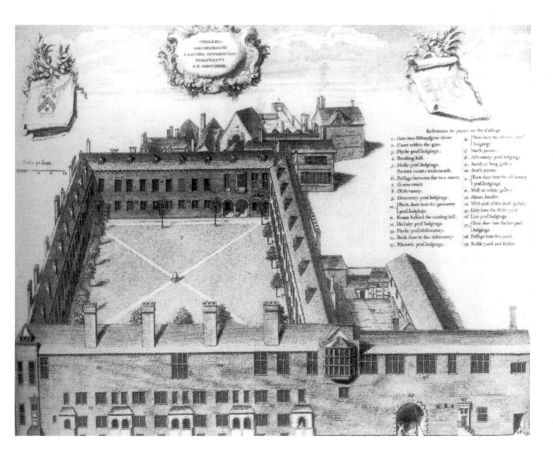

Gresham College.

Chief among them was John Wilkins, Royalist chaplain to the Elector Palatine (the husband of Charles' sister Elizabeth), who gained favour and the Wardenship of Wadham College, Oxford when his master threw in his lot with Parliament. Greatly respected for his personal charm and his dedication to excellence, he was to become the focus – in 'Parliamentary' Oxford – of an amazingly diverse group of scientists. Some, like Goddard (Cromwell's physician) and Petty, were Parliamentarians. Some, like Willis and Bathurst, were Royalists who had lost relatives in the Civil War. And some, like Wren and Hooke, were the talented but destitute offspring of disgraced Royalists who, instead of following their fathers into senior positions in the Church, came by various routes into Wilkin's 'Invisible College'.

In 1658, when hostilities had ended, many of these 'revolutionaries' returned to London, where the intellectual climate, the supply of books and the provision of equipment were better. Soon after, 'being much increased by the accession of divers noble persons, upon His Majesty's return we were about 1662 incorporated by the name The Royal Society'. The Society continued to meet at Gresham College, the City university founded by the Lord Mayor of that name, and in 'Mr Ball's chambers in the Temple'. But apart from providing some accommodation for a group of impoverished scientists, Gresham College had little to recommend it, for the intellectual climate was that of the main universities and it had no facilities for research. The search for a permanent base, which was to take the Society to three sites along the Thames, therefore became a matter of urgency. Initially it was hoped that the King, who had evinced some interest in science and had his own laboratory at Whitehall, might finance the venture. But apart from granting a charter, which among other things gave the Society the right to dissect the bodies of executed criminals and to publish without seeking episcopal permission, and sending the occasional gift of venison, Charles' interest seemed to dwindle. Indeed, he was heard to poke fun at the members of the Society, referring to them as his *fous* (jesters) who spent their time 'weighing ayre'. The 'divers noble persons' also failed to provide the hoped-for support, and the hard core of 'virtuosi' wasted much time in providing entertainment for these aristocratic associates.

At one stage it was suggested that the problem of accommodation might be resolved if the Fellows of the College of Physicians would allow the Society to use their rooms in Amen Corner. This was a vain hope, for although many Fellows of the College were also Fellows of the Society (one group had indeed established a Society of Chemical Physicians in the belief that 'there is no way to redeem our Profession but by setting the whole frame of Physick upon a new foot of Operative and Experimental Philosophy'), the College was rooted in the Oxbridge tradition. It therefore sympathised with the Public Orator at Oxford who had denounced the Royal Society and its new philosophy as 'men who can admire nothing but fleas, lice and themselves'. Moreover, it was unhappy about a group of amateur enthusiasts, described by the censor as 'swarmes of quackes, mountebacks, chymists, Apothecares and surgions' developing into a rival learned society. Nor was the College the only critic, for Church dignitaries had little time for the 'New Philosophy (as they call it) which was set on foot, and has been carried out by the ants of Rome, and those whose oath and interest is to maintain all her superstitions'. This widespread denunciation of the Society came to the notice of Hooke when he went to see Thomas Shadwell's play *The Virtuoso* at the Dorset Garden Theatre behind St Bride's and found, to his horror, that the character of Sir Nicholas Gimcrack, whose propensity for doing absurd experiments added a new word to the language, was based on himself.

Matters came to a head when, following the Great Fire, Gresham College was taken over by the Corporation and the Royal Exchange – the rooms belonging to Goddard, now their Professor of Physic, being commandeered by the City Chamberlain. Happily, through the good offices of Evelyn, alternative accommodation was found in Arundel House, the town house of the Earls of Arundel which stood near St Clement Danes between Strand Lane and Milford Street, on a site once occupied by the inn of the Bishops of Bath and Wells. (The 'Roman' Bath in Strand Lane may be a relic of this building.) Following the Reformation, this inn had been reconstructed by Thomas Seymour, brother of 'Protector' Somerset and husband of Henry's widow Catherine Parr (see Table 5) – a courtier whose unseemly 'romps' with his ward, the young Princess Elizabeth, led to his execution for treason in 1549. The house was bought for a mere £40 by Henry Fitzalan, twelfth Earl of Arundel, who had gained favour by being the only member of the Royal Council to vote against the succession of Lady Jane Grey and in favour of the Catholic Mary. However, when Elizabeth came to the throne, Philip, the thirteenth Earl, was confined to the Tower, where he died.

In 1607 Philip's son, Thomas, who had spent an impoverished childhood on the Continent, was restored to the title. Having abandoned Catholicism, he became Earl Marshal and (in the company of William Harvey) undertook diplomatic missions to the Continent. It was not long, however, before he too incurred the wrath of the King and was imprisoned for two years – ostensibly because he allowed his son to marry a royal ward, but probably because he supported those in the Lords who were attacking the King's favourite, Buckingham. But this 'Collector Earl' is mainly remembered as a patron of the arts. He entertained Wenceslaus Hollar, from whose magnificent drawings much of our knowledge of London is derived, and built up a vast collection of marbles and other treasures for which Inigo Jones designed an open-sided gallery that ran down towards the river.

'Roman' Bath, Strand Lane.

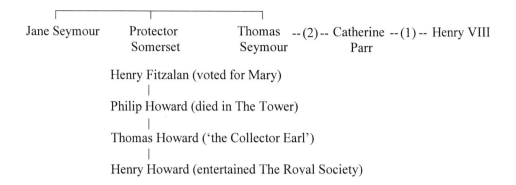

```
┌─────────────────┬──────────────┬────────────────────────────────────────┐
Jane Seymour      Protector      Thomas   --(2)-- Catherine --(1)-- Henry VIII
                  Somerset       Seymour          Parr
```

Henry Fitzalan (voted for Mary)
|
Philip Howard (died in The Tower)
|
Thomas Howard ('the Collector Earl')
|
Henry Howard (entertained The Royal Society)

Table 5. The Seymours and the Howards.

Arundel House, with old St Paul's in the distance. Note the end of the gallery (seen also on the etching on page 31) on the left of the picture. (Courtesy of the Guildhall Library, London)

During the Civil War, Thomas Howard fled to the Continent, taking much of his collection with him and putting it in the name of his Countess for safety. But the two became estranged, and as one part of his collection was being sold by his wife, the other was being vandalised by the troops occupying Arundel House. Thomas Howard died in exile and Henry Howard, the grandson who succeeded him, was an impoverished figure who was happy to offer the Royal Society a home to defray some of the cost of running Arundel House, or even to sell the Society enough land to build the longed-for headquarters on this site. Wren had indeed drawn up plans and some timber had been bought when it became evident that the project was unaffordable. But the Society continued to meet there, and for years the overworked Hooke had to transport all the equipment needed for demonstrations from Gresham College a mile and a half away.

The association with Arundel House was, however, marked by two important events. The first occurred in November 1667, when Lower and King, having heard that two French patients had been transfused with blood from a sheep, repeated this experiment for the first time in England. (The procedure was supposed to improve a defective memory, but when the authorities at Bedlam refused to supply a suitable recipient they were forced to find one – an Oxford graduate – for themselves.)

The second event of significance was the acquisition by the Society of the Arundel House library, a magnificent collection of books and manuscripts made by the Earl's grandfather. Evelyn, who engineered the bequest, felt it would 'preserve these documents from imbezilment', for the Earl, who was glad to be relieved of the cost of maintaining the library, had 'so little inclination to bookes' that he was giving them away in a haphazard manner. The transfer, however, was not without problems. Within ten years, and before the library had left Arundel House, the Earl complained that it was being neglected and that various Fellows were taking volumes out on long, and even indefinite, 'loan'. Hooke, the librarian, was among the offenders, and at one point the president threatened to confiscate his key. A second crisis occurred when, as agreed with the Earl (who was Earl Marshal), books on heraldry and genealogy were separated and sent to the College of Arms. Sir William Dugdale, who was appointed to oversee this task, had just lost his personal library in the Great Fire and Hooke suspected – not without cause – that he was setting aside books unrelated to heraldry that were to go elsewhere. The Earl agreed, and steps were taken to ensure that volumes selected for the College of Arms actually arrived there.

During this time, various schemes designed to provide a permanent base for the Society were being considered. A second attempt to join the College of Physicians, now rebuilding at Warwick Lane after the fire, was abandoned and a site offered by Charles II (eventually occupied by the Royal Hospital, Chelsea) could not be developed for lack of funds. It seemed indeed that the Society was destined to remain at Arundel House when, in 1673, it received a pressing invitation to return to Gresham College. The College had now reopened and the presence of the Society, apart from lending distinction to a struggling institution, would have provided it with a library (which it lacked) and excused those of its professors who were Fellows from paying membership fees. The remains of the great Arundel House collection were therefore broken up, the marbles going to Oxford (where they were 'sadly neglected') along with the manuscripts from the library, which the Society promptly sold off. Meanwhile Hooke trundled the remaining 3,000 volumes across London on carts to their new home in Gresham College. Arundel House itself was demolished in 1678 and is now the site of Arundel, Norfolk, Howard and Surrey Streets.

CRANE COURT

Conditions at Gresham were far from satisfactory due to the continuing presence of refugees from the fire but by 1702, when there was talk of the College being rebuilt, the Society was sufficiently well-established to submit a list of its requirements – including parking space for coaches, 'some of which are of very great quality'. Its presence in the College, however, depended on Hooke's right as a professor to have rooms there, and three weeks after his death in 1703 the members were told to remove their belongings and to return the keys forthwith. (There was a certain irony in this, for Newton, the new president, had refused to have anything to do with the organisation as long as Hooke was alive, yet his death immediately presented him with a crisis.) In the event, the Society contrived to remain at Gresham College for another eight years until a suitable alternative was found.

The task of finding new accommodation was given to Wren, who eventually discovered that the home of the late Dr Edward Browne, the son of Sir Thomas, was for sale. This building, No. 2 Crane Court, stood at the end of a close on the north side of Fleet Street 'in the middle of town out of noise'. The area had been developed by Barbon, who lived there, and although the building needed to be refurbished and a 'Repository of Curiosities' would have to be erected in the little paved courtyard at the rear it seemed to be an ideal choice. On this occasion, after some initial delay, funds were forthcoming, including an amazingly large donation from the technician in charge of the existing museum. This probably came from a chest containing over £8,000 that was found in Hooke's room after his death, for although he left no (signed) will it was known that he wanted to endow the Society to which he had devoted his life with a meeting room, laboratory, library and museum. It is also likely that, as his last professional task, Wren designed this Repository of Curiosities, 'a Theatrical building resembling that of Leyden in Holland', as a tribute to his lifelong colleague. Hooke's name, however, could not be mentioned in Newton's presence, and even his portrait and instruments vanished in the course of the move from Gresham College. Moreover, the comments of visitors suggest that the state of the exhibits

Royal Society building, Crane Court. (Courtesy of the Guildhall Library, London)

Right: Crane Court.

Below: Meeting room of the Royal Society, Crane Court.

P.Stopford del.   J.W.Lowry fc.

MEETING ROOM OF THE ROYAL SOCIETY, CRANE COURT.

John W. Parker, 445, West Strand, June 1848.

in the new museum left a great deal to be desired. But at long last the Society had a home of its own wherein, after dining at the Mitre on the other side of Fleet Street – or, in the case of Newton, Halley and Sloane, at the Grecian in Devereux Court (an inn favoured by the medical, scientific and legal communities, and by Sarah Mapp the bonesetter) – it held meetings which were advertised by a light hung over the entrance to Crane Court.

71

The Society remained in Crane Court until 1780, when it was offered new accommodation in Somerset House. Somerset House had long been used by the wives of various monarchs, but Queen Charlotte had chosen to remain in Buckingham Palace and by 1774 the elderly building was in a state of collapse. George III therefore ordered that it should be demolished and rebuilt to centralise government offices that were scattered all over London. He insisted, however, that the Strand front should be reserved for the three learned societies, the Royal Academy of Arts, the Society of Antiquaries and the Royal Society. Unfortunately, while the Academy of Arts had the whole of the western side of the building, members of the Royal Society were expected (as indicated by a sign which is still above the doorway) to share a common entrance and the eastern side with their fellow diners at the Mitre, the Society of Antiquaries. This provoked bitter

Above: Strand front of the new Somerset House, the fourth home of the Royal Society. (Courtesy of the Guildhall Library, London)

Left: The entrance shared by the Royal Society and the Royal Antiquarian Society, Somerset House. (Courtesy of Somerset House and Nick Wood Photography)

opposition, but although the Royal Society eventually obtained exclusive use of the porter's lodge it had to endure the lack of space until it moved to Burlington House in 1857. On a happier note, however, the location of the Royal Society just across the courtyard from the very powerful Navy Board meant that, during this important period, the latter had immediate access to advice about astronomy, navigation and various technological developments.

The Society should perhaps have considered itself fortunate that it received any favours from the King, with whom it had recently crossed swords. In 1764 the famous 'wedding cake' steeple of St Bride's (it is said that the idea of the tiered wedding cake was conceived by the master cook William Rich, when gazing at the steeple from his shop at No. 3 Ludgate Hill), the tallest in the City, had been struck by lightning. The advisability of fitting a lightning conductor was therefore considered and the Royal Society was consulted about the matter. There was good reason for this as one of its Fellows, Benjamin Franklin, had recently earned that distinction through an experiment in which he 'drew lightning from the clouds' – an exceedingly dangerous procedure (and one which he may not have actually carried out) that killed the next two people who tried it. A committee of five was therefore appointed to consider the matter, and it was hardly surprising that four followed Franklin's advice that such a conductor should have sharp terminals. But George III, who did not relish the idea of taking instructions from one of the colonial rebels with whom he was having so much trouble, was unwilling to accept this idea. He therefore sent for the president, who happened to be his personal physician, Sir John Pringle, and ordered him to have the decision reversed. Pringle's plea that he 'could not reverse the laws and operations of nature' fell on deaf ears and, having told him that in that case he was not fit to be president, the monarch departed to install blunt-ended conductors at the palace. Franklin's supporters retorted:

> While you, great George, for knowledge hunt
> And sharp conductors turn to blunt
> The nation's out of joint.
> Franklin a wiser course pursues
> And all your thunder useless views,
> By keeping to the point.

In fact George had the last word, for in a recent experiment a set of blunt receivers was struck twelve times over the course of seven years whereas a similar group of sharp receivers was not hit at all.

In view of the numerous acrimonious exchanges between the Royal College of Physicians and the Royal Society, it is worth concluding with a more felicitous link between the two. Men of learning in this period were, as we have seen, avid collectors of all manner of natural objects (see pages 57-59), and were anxious to have a pictorial record of their treasures. There was therefore a demand for artists who could produce such illustrations, and when Hans Sloane, president of both the Royal Society and of the College of Physicians, found that a certain George Edwards (1694-1773) had such a talent, he was eager to employ him. For his part, Edwards, seeing the commercial possibilities of the situation, 'resolved to mend my hand and my prices'. But better was to follow, for in 1733 the bedell at the College of Physicians died and Edwards was appointed in his place. This was an excellent opportunity, for it provided him with a salary, generous accommodation in the new College building in Warwick Lane and easy access to his customers both in the College and in the Royal Society building at Crane Court. Although, unlike his contemporary Stubbs, he does not appear to have done any anatomical work, over the next forty years Edwards produced a steady stream of other illustrations, most notably the books

One of George Edward's illustrations.
(Courtesy of the Royal College of Physicians)

on the natural history of birds that were to earn him the Copley Medal and Fellowship of the Royal Society. During part of this time, he lived in Clifford's Inn, Fleet Street.

8

'DOCTORS', PHYSICIANS AND SURGEONS

By the eighteenth century, the inns and coffee houses of Fleet Street had become the haunts of the intelligentsia. In particular, they were patronised by two 'doctors' and by three important medical societies which deserve special mention. Surgeons, however, were also working in the vicinity, and there is still evidence of body-snatching and of the schools of anatomy which once existed.

A century after producing Fleet Street's most famous patient, Salisbury Court was to become the haunt of its two most famous doctors. The first, Oliver Goldsmith (1728-1774), is somewhat of an enigma. Talented, generous and feckless, he certainly studied medicine at Dublin, Edinburgh, Leyden, Louvain and Padua and styled himself MB on the title-page of his poem 'The Traveller'. There is indeed no dispute that he had an *ad eundem* degree from Oxford, but it is doubtful whether he ever obtained an MB by examination. Certainly his attempts to practise – in London, with the East India Company or as a ship's surgeon – were a failure, and in order to survive he had to work as a reader and corrector in the Salisbury Court office of the great printer and author Samuel Richardson, whose memorial is in the crypt of St Bride's.

Whether or not he was qualified, Goldsmith retained an interest in medicine. He was a patron of Lettsom's Royal Humane Society and his writings give a vivid impression of the extent to which the impotence of orthodox medicine had allowed the growth of quackery. The number of charlatans at the Rainbow, near the gateway to the Inner Temple – whose proprietor was said to be 'making and selling a drink called coffee, whereby in making the same he annoyeth his neighbours by evil smells' – had indeed become so great that Addison christened it 'Quacks' Hall'. Such men never lost an opportunity to promote their nostrums, for, as one of Goldsmith's fictional characters observed, 'every wall is covered with their names, their abilities, their amazing cures and their places of abode. Before I was a week in town I was perfectly acquainted with the names of every great man or great woman of them all'. Their ingenuity knew no bounds. 'Dr' Rock, for example, had the effrontery to stop a carriage belonging to the King's physician Sir Edward Hulse in the middle of the Strand. Handing the coachman some boxes he said before an admiring crowd, 'Give my compliments to Sir Edward and tell him that these are all that I have, but I will send ten dozen more tomorrow'. Even Goldsmith himself was not averse to a little advertisement, for in one of his stories we are told that 'Margery's father was seized with a violent fever in a place where Dr James' powder was not to be had, and where he died miserably'. (James' powder was a powerful antimonial preparation that may have hastened the death of Walpole, of Sterne and indeed of Goldsmith himself. Its proprietor, Dr Robert James MD, was described as 'an uncouth character who spent his time with whores and had been drunk for twenty years'.)

Goldsmith, however, did make what could have been one very significant contribution to orthodox medicine, for he was probably the author of a review of a Viennese treatise entitled 'Inventum Novum' that appeared in the Public Ledger of 1761. The author was a man called Auenbrugger and the subject was the technique of percussion, a form of examination that was to be ignored by the medical profession for a further fifty years. Nor was he the only person in the district to consider the possibilities of physical examination, for the strange but brilliant Dr Robert Hooke, who used to meet his friend Thomas Tompion to discuss watches in a coffee house in Salisbury Square, asked in one of his many flashes of insight, 'Who knows but that one may discover the works performed in the several offices and shops of a man's body by the sound they make and thereby discover what instrument or engine is out of order'. It was to be another fifty years before the stethoscope was introduced.

The second 'doctor' to frequent Salisbury Court was Samuel Johnson (1709-1784), whose home was in Bolt Court at the other side of Fleet Street (near a statue of his cat Hodge and the oysters on which he was fed). Johnson, who for financial reasons left university without a degree, subsequently obtained honorary doctorates at Oxford and at Dublin, but these were of Letters. He was, however, very interested in medicine, had many doctors in his circle and collaborated with Dr James (an old schoolfellow, whose fever powder he mistrusted) in producing a medical dictionary. Like Wesley's *Primitive Physic*, this book was designed to make 'every man his own doctor', for Johnson would not accept that the art of healing was confined to the medical profession. Indeed he had little time for arrogant 'society' physicians, and dedicated the book to Richard Mead — one of the few physicians who advocated collaboration with the despised

Statue of Dr Johnson behind St Clement Danes.

76

Johnson's cat, Hodge – with oysters.

apothecaries. Johnson, however, went further still, and for twenty years gave a home to Robert Levet, an unqualified practitioner who learned his trade by hanging round the outskirts of medicine and practised in the slums of Marylebone and Houndsditch. As the only payment many of his patients could offer was a glass of gin, he was often drunk. Yet Johnson insisted that, if Levet was not present, he would not be satisfied with the advice of the whole College of Physicians, for:

> His vig'rous remedy display'd
> The power of art without the show.

THE MEDICAL SOCIETIES OF FLEET STREET

The fashionable area of Finsbury Square and Finsbury Pavement, near Hooke's great Bethlehem Hospital (whose similarity to the Tuileries in Paris so enraged Louis XIV that he had St James's Palace used as a model for 'some very inferior French offices'), was the Harley Street of eighteenth-century London, and in nearby Warwick Lane there was another of Hooke's buildings, the new College of Physicians. The control of medicine had long been in the hands of this College, whose duty it was to license those who wished to practise within seven miles of the City. It was run by a group of some forty Fellows – society physicians who, having been educated at Oxford or Cambridge, were by definition Anglicans. Inert but self-satisfied, they were eager to emphasise the fact that 'while there was a certain proportion of patients in this great town that we abandon to them,' the Licentiates of the College were 'no physicians, and stand in no other relationship to us than the publican does to the bench of justices from whom he receives a licence to sell beer'. In particular, they disliked graduates from Scotland, a country given to rebellion, whose new university at Edinburgh was producing 'men of mechanical education' who 'lacked the moral and intellectual qualities on which physicians pride themselves'. This was not an attitude that was likely to appeal to the 'needy adventurers' concerned, a group that included many of the most active and able physicians in town, and they in turn complained of their inability to influence the affairs of the College and of its 'mouldering library and empty halls'. When petitions and litigation failed to improve their lot, they repaired to bases in and around Fleet Street and adopted other methods.

First to appear was the eminently respectable Society of Physicians, founded by John Fothergill in 1752 for 'those who have the care of hospitals or are otherwise in some degree of repute in their profession'. The membership of the Society was indeed distinguished, for at one time six of the seven were also Fellows of the Royal Society. It held its meetings on alternate Mondays in the Mitre, a well-known inn on the south side of Fleet Street that was Dr Johnson's 'base' and was frequented by Goldsmith and by Pepys. (It was also one of the places where Radcliffe saw patients and was used by the Royal Society, by the Society of Antiquaries and later by Thomas Hodgson, a 'retired' body-snatcher from Leeds, who 'held consultations' there. The inn has now been demolished but the site is marked by a blue plaque on the wall of Hoare's Bank; Hoare's other claim to fame is that he paid for the Westminster, London's first subscription hospital, in 1719.) The Society of Physicians published its deliberations (at Fothergill's expense) in its *Medical Observations and Inquiries* – a journal which, according to one enthusiastic member,

Above left: The Mitre tavern, Fleet Street. (Courtesy of the Guildhall Library, London)

Above right: Site of the Mitre.

'communicated to the world more useful information than the College has done in its corporate capacity since the time of its first foundation'.

On 16 January 1767 a second medical society, the Society of Collegiate Physicians, held its inaugural meeting at the Crown and Anchor in Arundel Street, opposite St Clement Danes (an inn which was also patronised by political agitators, by the Royal Society and by the Society of Apothecaries). Once more it consisted of Licentiates who had been refused access to the College, and among the thirty people present were such prominent figures as Fothergill and William Hunter. The objective of this Society (apart from meeting to dine at the Crown four times a year) was supposedly 'to promote the Science of Physic and thereby the honour of the Profession in General'. Almost at once, however, its members firmly rejected an invitation to contribute to *Medical Transactions*, a journal which the College had been stung into producing by the success of Fothergill's *Medical Observations*. Instead, to the delight of the cartoonists and the horror of the president, some of the wilder spirits literally smashed their way into a meeting of the Senate at the College in Warwick Lane 'like swimming sea monsters in our medical ocean'. Subsequently, the Society continued to meet at the Crown and Anchor and at Old Slaughter's – an inn in St Martin's Lane favoured by artists – but by degrees it degenerated into a dining club more concerned with the consumption of Fothergill's turtle soup than with revolutionary medical politics.

The Crown and Anchor, Fleet Street.
(Courtesy of the Guildhall Library, London)

The Battle between the Fellows & Licenciates.

The invasion of the College of Physicians by the Licentiates. (Courtesy of the Royal College of Physicians)

Old Slaughter's tavern. (Courtesy of the British Museum)

The third, and in many ways the most important, group was the Society in Crane Court (later the Medical Society of London), which appeared in 1773. Like the Society of Physicians, it was founded by a Quaker, John Coakley Lettsom. Quakers, who had flourished after the Civil War as a result of the greater toleration extended to them and to Roman Catholics by James II, were part of an international organisation renowned for its industry and integrity. Devoid of class consciousness, they were devoted to the acquisition and dissemination of knowledge and the improvement of society, and found in medicine a profession ideally suited to their inclinations. Not being Anglicans, they were of course excluded from the English universities (and therefore from the College) and, to a large extent, from the hospital service which, at long last, was starting to develop. The hospital service, however, was far from satisfactory, for it was designed primarily for those in work, and in many instances children, pregnant women, those with infections, the chronic sick and the aged were specifically excluded. It was in an attempt to help such patients that the Dispensary Movement was started.

Dispensaries, which provided an outpatient and domiciliary service for the poor, were first introduced by the College in the latter part of the seventeenth century and by the evangelist John Wesley in the first half of the eighteenth. But it was with the foundation of the Aldersgate Street Dispensary by Lettsom in 1770 that the movement really became established, and by the end of the century there were fourteen such organisations in London alone. The physicians, surgeons and apothecaries working in these institutions saw vast numbers of patients in clinics or in their homes and were in an ideal position to study, and to teach, medicine and public health. It was, moreover, an occupation suited to the ideals of egalitarianism, service and education espoused by Quakers, and it was they who to a large extent staffed these valuable but somewhat despised buildings.

This development had an important bearing on the Society in Crane Court. The medical services of the time were fragmented, for physicians regarded themselves as superior to surgeons and both groups looked down on the apothecaries. It has therefore been suggested that Lettsom, who insisted that his Society should consist of equal numbers of all three, was simply trying to heal this breach. But as recent commentators have pointed out, these parties were already working together harmoniously in the dispensaries. The real problem was that there was no forum in which the staff from different institutions could meet and exchange ideas, for 'ordinary' physicians and surgeons were not welcome in their respective Colleges and the apothecaries were not welcome in either. Lettsom, therefore, was not trying to outshine the College, to enforce the rights of Licentiates or to found a dining club. Rather, for academic purposes, he was trying to establish a permanent meeting place with a library and museum for those working in dispensaries scattered round London. Nor was this his only philanthropic venture, for he also founded the Royal Sea Bathing Society – designed to give the poor access to a form of treatment which was in vogue – and (with William Hawes, an apothecary of Palsgrave Place in the Strand) the Royal Humane Society for 'resuscitation of the apparently drowned' by various means, including (in 1788) electric shocks to the heart.

In 1774, after meeting for a time in the Crown and Anchor and various other taverns, the Society rented one of the houses in Crane Court, near the home of the Royal Society. Its early meetings were not without incident, for on one occasion the president locked the Society out of its own rooms and in 1780 the building was damaged during the Gordon Riots. Moreover, when the Royal Society moved to Somerset House, Crane Court lost something of its distinction and by 1786 it seemed that the Society would be destroyed by a fall in membership. Inspired by Lettsom's generosity in donating a new home, however, it moved eastwards to another alley on the north side of Fleet Street and became known as the Society in (No. 3) Bolt Court behind the Bolt in Tun inn.

THE ROYAL JENNERIAN SOCIETY

It was at this stage that the Society became involved in the implementation of one of the great medical discoveries of the eighteenth century. London was still seeing some 12,000 cases of smallpox each year but in 1721 Lady Mary Wortley Montagu, wife of the British Consul in Constantinople, had introduced the Turkish technique of preventing major attacks by inducing mild infections with small amounts of matter from smallpox lesions. Although not without its dangers, this procedure was effective and the Medical Society of London soon became

Left: House in Crane Court. (Courtesy of the Guildhall Library, London)

Above: Bolt Court, Fleet Street.

Below left: The Bolt in Tun inn, Fleet Street. (Courtesy of the Guildhall Library, London)

Below right: The Society in Bolt Court. (Courtesy of the Medical Society of London)

an enthusiastic advocate of the technique. But in 1795 John Adams, a future president of the Society, pointed out that it was also known that 'a person who has been infected with cowpox is rendered insensible to the variolous (smallpox) poison'. This was a year before Jenner, an obscure country general practitioner, began to experiment with this technique and three years before he published his results. By 1798 Jenner was in London, trying, without much success, to publicise his book, his paper on the subject having been rejected by the Royal Society. It was at this stage that the president of the Medical Society of London, recognising the importance of his work, invited him to speak. He did so in 1800 and although the reception was not entirely favourable (one member was disgusted by the idea of transmitting 'acrid animal poisons' to man) most were enthusiastic.

Jenner could hardly have found a better way of disseminating his ideas, for the Society, with its vast national and international connections, was in an ideal position to promote vaccination. Indeed, one enthusiast suggested that vaccination and baptismal certificates should be issued together. The headquarters of the campaign, the Royal Jennerian Society, was established opposite Bolt Court at No. 14 Salisbury Square and within a year nearly 7,000 Londoners had been vaccinated. Sadly, however, there was a clash between the resident inoculator Dr John Walker and the president of the Society, and Walker resigned. He then set up a private establishment in Salisbury Square that waylaid would-be patients before they reached the Jennerian Society and, shortly after, the latter had to be closed.

The Society in Bolt Court remained there until 1850 when, due to the decline of the City as a social and residential area, it was once more faced with a fall in membership. It therefore amalgamated with the Westminster, another medical society that was experiencing similar problems and, adopting the name of the Medical Society of London, moved westwards to George Street, Hanover Square. (Those remaining in the City formed the John Hunter Society which, after meeting in various coffee houses, took to meeting in the London Press Centre in Fleet Street and to dining at the Savoy.) In 1907, under Osler's benign influence, the majority of London's medical societies united to form the Royal Society of Medicine. Lettsom's society refused to join because it was felt that apothecaries (i.e. general practitioners) were not adequately represented; it is therefore the oldest medical society in London.

EXETER HOUSE

While the members of the Royal Society were conducting their scientific experiments in Arundel House, a different approach to learning was being pursued by another group of Oxford physicians nearby. Exeter House, which stood on the opposite side of the Strand on the site of the Strand Palace Hotel, was now the home of Lord Ashley, later the Earl of Shaftesbury – a politician who had contrived to hold office under Charles I, Parliament and Charles II. During a visit to Oxford to 'take the waters', Ashley encountered a young man called John Locke (1632-1704), one of the many distinguished products of Busby's Westminster School. Locke had made little impact at Oxford, although he was on the fringes of Wilkins' 'Invisible College' and had carefully recorded the lectures of Thomas Willis. Ashley, however, was more impressed with Locke's philosophical ideas, with which he was in sympathy, and it was for this reason that he invited him to come to Exeter House as his physician and (later) political mentor.

Although Locke was not renowned as a physician, he obtained some publicity when he opened a large swelling that had developed on Lord Ashley's abdomen, thus releasing a mass of small cysts – presumably from a tapeworm. The wound was kept open to allow it to drain and Locke invited Thomas Willis, his Oxford tutor, to examine his patient. (Willis had moved to St Martin's Lane in 1666 at the instigation of his patron Archbishop Sheldon, and soon became so busy that he hardly ever attended meetings of the Royal Society.) Locke, however, had reservations about the value of the anatomical and physiological studies conducted by Willis and his colleagues, and was not alone in thinking that they contributed little to clinical practice. He was more in sympathy with the teaching of Thomas Sydenham (1624-1672), another contemporary from Oxford who, unlike Willis (who was a Royalist), had served with the Parliamentary cavalry. Consequently, while Willis was enjoying the benefits of the Restoration, Sydenham had fallen from favour and was reduced to working among the poor. But this extensive practice allowed him to make the important observation that 'disease' was not, as was generally believed, a disequilibrium of the humours of the body peculiar to each individual, but that groups of patients, presumably with the same condition, developed the same characteristic symptoms and signs. He therefore began to classify these different diseases, just as, in his Oxford days, he had classified different species of plants. He also realised that his patients often recovered more rapidly if, instead of administering the noxious drugs then in vogue, he simply supported them while the illness was allowed to run its natural course. Unlike his 'learned' colleagues, he made no pretence of understanding the nature of these diseases and saw no virtue in anatomical and physiological studies.

In the circumstances of the time, this simple approach was indeed of more practical value than Willis' painstaking dissections and ingenious experiments. It was to be the inspiration for the great medical schools at Leyden and Edinburgh and was to earn Sydenham the epitaph of 'A physician famous for all time'. But for Locke it was also confirmation of a philosophical idea with which he had grappled for years. He could accept that the mind was in some way associated with the brain but could not see how anatomical studies and scientific arguments could determine its exact location or the way in which it worked. Indeed, like Sydenham, whose methods he studied and with whom he worked, he came to believe that there were many things which were beyond the reach of the human mind. These musings were, however, interrupted when his patron, who had been plotting against the succession of the Catholic Duke of York, had to flee the country. Locke, who was known to be his confidant, also had to go into exile for eight years, during which time his ideas were expounded in his influential *Essay Concerning Human Understanding*.

SURGERY

The College of Physicians was not the only group of doctors whose members were dissatisfied with its performance. Despite having a magnificent lecture theatre modelled on the one in Padua, teaching at what was still the Company of Barber Surgeons was so inadequate that members were setting up rival schools of anatomy. In 1714, for example, there was a complaint that William Cheselden 'did frequently procure the bodies of dead malefactors' and 'dissect them in his own house as well during the Company's publick lectures as at other times'. But Cheselden clearly had the welfare of the Company at heart, for he eventually resigned from St Thomas's and, after holding various offices, was instrumental in establishing the independent Company of Surgeons in 1745.

With such talented and dynamic leadership, it seemed that the new Company had a bright future, but this promise was not fulfilled. The lecture theatre was not replaced promptly and an opportunity to establish a museum with the help of William Hunter was turned down. The old system of apprenticeship was replaced by a rather superficial examination and, apart from feasting and promoting their own careers, the officers appeared to do very little. Eventually, in 1790, in what became known as Gunning's Philippic, a new master told his colleagues:

You have instituted lectures neither in surgery nor indeed in anatomy of any importance. Your theatre is without lectures, your library without books is converted into an office for your clerk and your committee room is become an eating parlour. If you make no better use of your Hall you had better sell it.

In view of these comments, it seems strange that Gunning should have been one of a group that resisted John Hunter's attempts to modernise the practice and teaching of surgery at St George's Hospital.

Under such circumstances it was hardly surprising that private schools of anatomy, along with the body-snatchers on whom their activities depended, continued to flourish. Evidence of this can still be seen in the crypt of St Clement Danes, where there is one of the chains with which coffins were bound in an attempt to protect them. An even more interesting relic can be found on the west side of Surrey Street, to the south of the church. Down an alley marked 'To the Roman Bath' (actually a relic of the inn of the Bishop of Bath and Wells which once stood on this site, or possibly of the garden of Arundel House) can be found an elegant house with a wrought-iron balcony. Known as the Old Watch House, it served as a lookout post from which the graveyard now under King's College could be guarded. Among the establishments supplied by local body-snatchers were Frank Nicholl's school in Clare Market (now covered by Kingsway), where Hunter complained that he got no practical experience during his training, and Hunter's own school in the piazza on the northwest corner of Covent Garden.

Left: The Old Watch House, Strand Lane

Above: Coffin chain in the crypt of St Clement Danes.

More recently, evidence of a third school in the vicinity has come to light. During the course of alterations at No. 36 Craven Street (on the west side of Charing Cross station) workmen uncovered a pit containing human remains. There was one complete body, that of a child, and 1,500 other parts coming from at least twenty other corpses. From trephine holes in the skulls and the way in which the long bones were cut across, it was evident that these were relics from a school of anatomy. At first it was thought that Franklin, who lodged at this address, might have been responsible but although Franklin had a considerable interest in medicine this does not seem to have included anatomy. Eventually it transpired that the person responsible was William Hewson (1739-1774).

Hewson, who is reputed to be the man dissecting the eye on the well-known print of an anatomy school, was the son of an apothecary in Hexham. He trained at Guy's and St Thomas's and in Hunter's school of anatomy, and his reputation is derived largely from Hunter's work on the lymphatics, which he demonstrated by injecting them with mercury. It had been suggested that the lymphatics played a part in digestion but this idea was challenged because no such system had been found in birds. Hewson was able to show that there was a lymphatic system in birds, reptiles and fish – studies which earned for him both the Fellowship and the Copley Medal of the Royal Society.

Hewson appears to have been a model pupil and during John Hunter's absence on military service he was left in charge of the anatomy school in Covent Garden. He then went into partnership with William Hunter – an agreement that came to an acrimonious end, probably because Hewson had married and was no longer available to supervise the school at all hours. There was then a dispute as to whether he should be allowed to remove his own anatomical preparations and Franklin was called in to arbitrate. Franklin knew both of the parties involved, Hewson because his wife, Mary Stevenson, was the daughter of Franklin's landlady at No. 36 Craven Street, and it was here that Hewson subsequently established his own school.

No. 36 Craven Street.

Above: Cartoon of dissecting room. The student operating on the eye is said to be Hewson. (Courtesy of the Royal College of Physicians)

Right: William Hewson. (Courtesy of the Royal College of Physicians)

The building was reconstructed to provide a lecture theatre and a museum, and 'all the leading men of science' were invited to the inaugural lecture in 1772. It subsequently proved to be so popular that it attracted more than half the pupils from Hunter's school in Windmill Street but its success was short-lived, for in 1774 Hewson died of a wound contracted during a dissection. His funeral took place in St Martin in the Fields and his effects were subsequently disposed of in a series of sales that attracted much attention. One item of particular interest was 'An elegant mahogany inlaid cabinet with 16 drawers containing about 300 microscopical objects, spread upon glass and enclosed in glass tubes hermetically sealed'. This collection, made at a time when microscopy had still had little impact on medicine, was evidently shared between John Hunter and Jenner. The 1850 catalogue of the Histological Series in the Royal College of Surgeons records that the nucleus of its collection is '150 specimens prepared by William Hewson' – presumably Hunter's share of these slides.

9

THE PRESS

At the end of the fifteenth century, exponents of the new art of printing were drawn to Fleet Street by the fact that the Church – which was almost alone in having the money to buy and the skill to read printed material – was heavily represented in that area. Over the years, as clerics were replaced by scientists, artists and philosophers and then by the world of commerce, Fleet Street publishers continued to find new customers and to flourish until, after 500 years, the last representatives of the press – the great newspapers – moved to a new site.

From its earliest years, Fleet Street has been a market for the exchange of ideas and information. Before the arrival of Caxton's disciple, Wynkyn de Worde, in 1500 it was already the home of members of the Companies of Scriveners (who copied books) and Limners (who illustrated them). Like de Worde these organisations had been attracted by the concentration of monasteries and episcopal dwellings in the area. So great was the demand for such services that other printers soon appeared and within thirty years there were at least six in Fleet Street. In 1557 their proprietors, who at this time were booksellers as well as publishers and printers, were incorporated as the Guild of Stationers – an allusion to the 'stations' or stalls from which they sold their wares. Such stations were to be found at Temple Bar, on Cheapside, in St Paul's

The Wynkyn de Worde memorial, Stationers' Hall, Ludgate Hill.

Fleet Street looking west. The lantern of the Mitre is on the left and the arch of Temple Bar, a popular site for stationers, is in the distance. On the right is the churchyard of St Dunstan's in the West, where Marriot published the *London Pharmacopoeia*.

churchyard and in Paternoster Row – an area previously occupied by the Beadmakers who had been put out of business by the Reformation. These establishments were not bookshops in the modern sense, however, for the pages were loose and a customer would sit at one of the desks provided, or even take manuscripts home to read them, before confirming a purchase by having them bound in whatever style he favoured.

The introduction of printing, which facilitated the dissemination of (potentially undesirable) ideas, was viewed with apprehension by both Government and Church, and the incorporation of the Company of Stationers was but one step in a long and unsuccessful campaign to contain this threat. It was Queen Mary who bestowed on its Freemen the (supposedly) exclusive right to publish without royal permission and an obligation to burn books condemned by the Bishop of London. The Company also kept a register of books published by its members – the earliest form of copyright – and it was this registration that prevented the College of Physicians from regulating the sale of the first *London Dispensary* (see page 40).

As a result of these and other restrictions, many authors took to using publishers on the Continent, where the press had a much greater degree of freedom. Others responded differently, and in works such as Milton's *Areopagitica* and Locke's *Essay Concerning Toleration* campaigned for greater freedom of speech. The abolition of licensing in 1694 did not, however, imply that their arguments had been accepted. Measures to control them had indeed failed but unwary publishers were still liable to be fined, imprisoned or even, on occasions, executed. The Puritan William Prynne, for example, whose gravestone now forms part of the floor of the undercroft of Lincoln's Inn (Slab No. 44) had his ears cut off and was branded for publishing criticism of the theatricals of which the Queen, Henrietta Maria, was so fond.

To protect the interests of its members, the Company of Stationers insisted that when 1,250 copies of a book had been printed the type was to be broken up. The price of books was therefore high and authors were poorly rewarded – Hogarth, whose father died struggling to produce a Latin dictionary, wrote of the 'cruel treatment he met with from booksellers and printers'. As a result, most writers followed Edmund Spenser, who depended on the Earl of Leicester, in seeking the support of a wealthy patron. But the standard of the printing left much to be desired, as is shown by the many notorious errors in different versions of the Bible. Thus in the Wicked Bible, produced by the King's Printers in Printing House Square (on the site of the old Blackfriars Monastery), the seventh commandment ordained that 'Thou shalt commit adultery' – an error for which the Star Chamber imposed a massive fine of £3,000. A clergyman looking for his text in another edition was even more unfortunate, for as he prepared to preach in St Paul's he found that the relevant verses had been entirely omitted – an error which led to the suggestion that the printing of Bibles should be left in the safe hands of the Cambridge University Press.

NEWS

In its early years, the London press spent much of its time producing small documents. Ballads were very popular as a means of conveying news, scandal, advice and disreputable stories; handbills recorded remarkable events like the recovery of William Duell, hanged at Tyburn in November 1770; and people like Baldwin Hamey junior of the College of Physicians, who had developed an intense dislike of the new Royal Society, would employ pamphleteers to present their cases. Eventually, by amalgamating and formalising such activities, Fleet Street came to concentrate on its main task, the dissemination of news.

London had always had a passion for news. As early as the sixteenth century, handbills were being sold from door to door, and by 1622 it had a paper which appeared (almost) every week. It was, however, forbidden to discuss affairs of Church or State and when this embargo was extended to include even foreign news the journal was forced out of business. But following the Civil War, when both Crown and Church lost their powers of censorship, there was a marked increase in the number of pamphlets and 'news books' published. Most notable among these was the *Oxford Gazette*, which was founded as a source of official information while the Court was in Oxford (because of the plague) but which, after being renamed the *London Gazette*, went on to become the most reliable and long-lived of London's many newspapers.

During the eighteenth century, the supply of newspapers and magazines became one of the great attractions of the new coffee houses that were appearing all over London. These journals were studied avidly by people from every rank of society, and visitors commented on the hush that fell over the room after the papers had been delivered. By 1702, as a plaque on the north side of the entrance to Ludgate Hill reminds us, London had a daily paper, the *Daily Courant* (a facility for which Paris would have to wait another seventy-five years), and the production of journals was being timed to coincide with the departure of coaches so that the same service could be extended to the provinces. By the end of the century, the City had 278 different newspapers

Plaque on Ludgate Hill commemorating the
Daily Courant, London's first daily newspaper.

and magazines and the list of proprietors included distinguished writers such as Defoe, Steele
and Addison. In certain quarters, however, they were still viewed with suspicion. Sheridan, for
example, observed: 'The newspapers! Sir, they are the most villainous – licentious – abominable
– infernal – not that I ever read them – no – I make it a rule never to look into a newspaper.'

With the introduction of power-driven presses in 1814, this seemingly endless growth
continued and between 1801 and 1831 the sale of newspapers (which from 1788 included *The
Times*) rose from 16 million to 30 million. By the end of the century, the mass readership of the
Daily Mail, presided over by the Harmsworth brothers, had made it the most potent medium
for advertisement yet devised. But the papers also played a much more serious role, for the
financial, political and commercial information they contained was the basis of business activity
in the City. There was, therefore, much sadness when these great institutions abandoned Fleet
Street, which had been their home for 500 years, and moved to Canary Wharf – a migration
undertaken in part to reduce the power of the 'guilds' (now unions) which were an essential
part of their history.

BOOKS AND MAGAZINES

The emphasis on newsprint tends to obscure the fact that Fleet Street, the home of publishers
such as Richardson (whose grave is in St Bride's) and John Murray, was once responsible for
the production of most of the great books in the English language. Playwrights, who feared
that audiences would fall if their work appeared in print, were something of an exception and
– except when the theatres were closed – they tended to avoid this relatively unrewarding
medium. Churches, on the other hand, were a fruitful source of business, for apart from the
great 1604 Authorised Version of the Bible they were endlessly proclaiming their various points
of view. So serious was this problem that Bishop Tunstall warned his colleagues that, 'We must
root out printing or printing will root us out'. Novelists also were good customers and it was
in a hovel near St Bride's that Johnson found Goldsmith about to be arrested for debt. Being
virtually destitute himself, he asked his friend if he had anything that he could sell. Producing a
bundle of papers, Goldsmith replied hesitantly, 'Well, there is this'. 'This' was the manuscript of
The Vicar of Wakefield.

Medical publishing followed the same general pattern, although medical texts, being 'learned',
were initially printed in Latin – a custom that died out during the course of the eighteenth

century. Initially, medical authors shared the same fear that their new ideas would offend the authorities and for this reason many texts (like Harvey's *De Motu Cordis*) were printed on the Continent. The eighteenth century, however, saw the publication of the first significant contributions to therapeutics in the form of books by Withering (on digitalis), Jenner (on vaccination) and Lind (on scurvy). Medical articles (initially in Latin) were also published in the *Philosophical Transactions of the Royal Society*, which first appeared in 1665. There was indeed a phase in which the Society was largely in the hands of doctors, whose publications left a great deal to be desired – a problem which was remedied in the middle of the eighteenth century when, for the first time, articles were submitted to a panel of assessors on which the medical profession was represented by Heberden. The first purely medical journal was founded in Edinburgh in 1731, to be followed in 1757 by Fothergill's *Medical Observations and Inquiries*, in 1767 by the College of Physicians' *Medical Transactions* and in 1773 by the *Journal of the Medical Society of London*, the oldest medical journal in existence. *The Lancet* first appeared in 1823 and the *Provincial Medical and Surgical Journal* (later to become the *British Medical Journal*) in 1840.

10

DURHAM HOUSE, THE ADELPHI AND THE EMBANKMENT

The operation to recover the muddy northern bank of the Thames took place in two stages. In the late eighteenth century, Durham House was replaced by the Adelphi – an area associated with 'Dr' James Graham and with The Lancet. This was followed a century later by the building of the Embankment – a project which, despite being based on a false premise, rid the City of cholera.

'Dr'. William Butler, a successful but unqualified seventeenth-century practitioner, who is reputed to have been consulted by Mayerne about the treatment of James I's son, Prince Henry, had rooms in the Savoy. On one occasion, anticipating the arrival of a particularly irritating patient, he stationed a boat below his window and when, as usual, the man had talked for some time he had him seized and thrown into the river. The story (and the claim that the patient was cured) are of course apocryphal but do make the point that, before the building of the Embankment in 1867, places like Hewson's house in Craven Street and Pepys' house in Buckingham Street were very close to the Thames.

The old boundary of the river is in fact clearly marked at several points. Behind the War Office a flight of steps built by Wren in 1691 runs down from a fragment of the waterside terrace of the old Palace of Whitehall. To the east of Charing Cross underground station the York Watergate (1626), the only bit of York House left by Barbon's development, stands at the back of Embankment Gardens. Somerset House, designed by Chambers in 1775 to accommodate (among other things) the Navy Board, has a huge arch through which the Controller's barge, which is still there, could sail when it took him to the Admiralty, to Westminster or to the dockyards. And on the site of Essex House, hastily demolished by Barbon before the King could claim it for a favourite, is another set of stairs which ran down to the river from the end of Essex Street.

DURHAM HOUSE

Since the building of the Embankment, these watergates and stairs have of course been left standing some distance away from the edge of the river. But the Embankment was not the first

River steps from the terrace of the old Palace of Whitehall, behind the War Office.

The York Watergate. York Buildings (Pepys' house) is on the left and the Adelphi, Waterloo Bridge and Somerset House are on the right. (Courtesy of the Museum of London)

A memorial to the Camel Corps, Embankment Gardens.

attempt to colonise the muddy banks of the Thames, for in 1772 Durham House became the site of the Adelphi, one of the finest property developments London had yet seen. Durham House, which was built for the Bishops of Durham in the thirteenth century and stood to the east of York House, had had an eventful life. At one time it had been the home of Simon de Montfort and, following the death of her first husband, Catherine of Aragon, the sixteen-year-old Princess Dowager of Wales, lived here in poverty until, seven years later, her future was decided by the death of Henry VII (see page 20). It had been owned by Wolsey, by Anne Boleyn (who used it to conspire with Cranmer about Henry's divorce) and by the Princess Elizabeth but by 1553 it had passed into the hands of John Dudley, Duke of Northumberland.

At Dudley's instigation, the great see of Durham had been broken up and Bishop Tunstall (along with a suffragan who was 'neither preacher, learned nor honest') had been deprived of his appointment. Such confiscation of Church property was popular with religious radicals, particularly when, as here, the incumbent was resistant to reforms. It was also seen as a means of replenishing the treasury at the expense of an organisation which, despite the Dissolution, was still worth an estimated £3.5 million. The acquisition of the castle and the Church land allowed Dudley, who was Warden General of the Marches, to improve the security of the border with Scotland and, incidentally, provided him with a magnificent mansion on the Thames. It was here that one of the great dramas of English history was to be enacted.

Edward VI (1547-1553) was a well-educated, intelligent and healthy youth, deeply committed to the Protestant cause. At the age of fifteen, however, he had a severe attack of what was probably measles, and thereafter there was a steady deterioration in his condition. According to Henry's instructions, if Edward died he was to be succeeded by the Catholic Princess Mary – a prospect which filled Northumberland and the other Protestant reformers with alarm. According to the usual version of the story, Northumberland therefore reopened the question of whether Mary and Elizabeth were legitimate, hinted that Mary had used witchcraft to cause Edward's illness and pointed out that, if Elizabeth was forced to marry a Catholic husband, the Protestant Reformation would be destroyed. With great reluctance, Edward and the Council

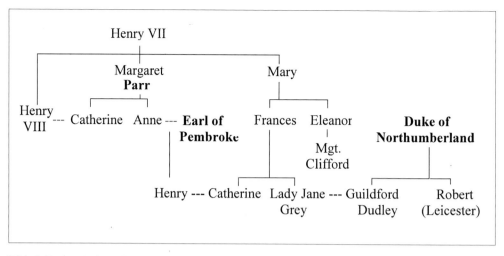

Table 6. Northumberland, Pembroke and the Lady Jane Grey conspiracy.

therefore agreed that Henry's instructions should be disregarded and that Mary and Elizabeth should be bypassed in favour of Henry's next choice, the descendants of his favourite younger sister Mary, Duchess of Suffolk. To capitalise on this situation, Northumberland then arranged for his sixth son Guildford to marry Edward's putative successor, Lady Jane Grey, a great-niece of Henry VIII and the daughter of his ally the Duke of Suffolk. But Lady Jane, a spirited fifteen-year-old, rebelled at the idea of marrying a conceited, spoilt, disagreeable young man who made no secret of the fact that he disliked her, and had to be beaten into submission. As an additional precaution, Northumberland also arranged for Lady Jane's younger sister Catherine to marry the son of Northumberland's (supposed) supporter, the Earl of Pembroke, in a double wedding which took place in Durham House on Whit Sunday 1553.

Northumberland, however, had misjudged the situation. Mary (1553-1558), who ignored an order to come to the bedside of the dying Edward, took refuge with the Catholic Norfolks, and although only one member of the Council voted in her favour (the Catholic Henry Fitzalan, who was subsequently allowed to buy Arundel House for £40), it soon became evident that Northumberland and his nominee were not popular. The Privy Council and the City went along with popular feeling and a few days later Mary entered the City in triumph. Northumberland's 'ally' Pembroke celebrated the accession and, having made certain that his son's marriage was not consummated, he quickly arranged a divorce. (In later years the unfortunate Catherine, by now next in line to the throne, incurred the wrath of Elizabeth when she married in secret. She and her husband were sent to the Tower, where she died, and her husband was fined £15,000 for seducing a royal virgin. To prevent the children from inheriting the throne, the marriage was annulled by the Archbishop of Canterbury.) William Cecil, Somerset's secretary, who had deserted him in favour of Northumberland, deftly changed sides yet again and continued his illustrious career. But for Northumberland there was no escape. Confessing that charges against the Duke of Somerset had been false and claiming that he was after all a Catholic – a devastating blow to the Protestant cause – he, along with Lady Jane, her husband and her father, was executed.

There is, however, another version of this story which puts matters in a different light. In 1552, as Derek Wilson points out, Edward VI appeared to be in good health and there was every reason to believe that he would develop into a wise and learned monarch. At this juncture, had Northumberland wished to promote his family, his obvious course would have been to engineer a marriage between his daughter and the King and between his son and Lady Jane Grey. In fact he arranged the betrothal of his daughter to the son and heir of another evangelical Councillor, the Earl of Huntingdon, and tried to arrange a marriage between his son Guildford and Lady Jane's younger cousin, Margaret Clifford. It was only when this proved to be impossible that Guildford was engaged to Lady Jane, whose sister Catherine was engaged to Pembroke's son Lord Herbert.

These arrangements, which would have united four leading families (and two claimants to the throne) in a tight evangelical alliance, would have been known to and approved of by Edward who, by this time, (perhaps because he was aware of the severity of his illness) was wrestling in secret with the problem of the succession. He required a male Protestant heir and among his various relatives no such person existed. He therefore gave written instructions that, in the event of his death, Mary and Elizabeth should be set aside and that the throne should pass to the male heir of his cousin Frances Brandon or, failing that, of her daughters Lady Jane, Lady Catherine and Lady Mary or of their cousin Margaret Clifford. This absurd scheme, which would have required a regency until such time as the child (as yet unborn) came of age, was unknown to the families that met in Durham House for what was in fact a triple wedding in May 1553.

A month later, when the gravity of Edward's illness and his unworkable plans for the succession became known, his Councillors were aghast. But Cranmer, the one person who dared to question them, was severely rebuked and, as usual, his colleagues looked to Northumberland for advice. Only then did he realise that, by making a minute alteration to Edward's document so that the phrase 'Lady Jane's heirs male' read 'Lady Jane and her heirs male', he could obtain a young, intelligent Protestant Queen and preserve his authority and all that he had been working for. But the sequence of events and his uncharacteristically inept handling of the situation show that this was not a preconceived plan. Failing to make allowances for opposition from colleagues, for his unpopularity in the country and for a surge of sympathy and support for Mary, Northumberland was swept from power and used by erstwhile colleagues as token propitiation for treason that was not of his making. Confined in the Tower, where the full canon of the Mass had been restored, he received the elements at the hands of the once excluded Bishop Gardiner and, to the horror of his Protestant colleagues, re-embraced the Catholic faith. He was buried beside his rival Somerset before the altar of St Peter ad Vincula in the Tower.

DR JOHN DEE

It seems almost certain that among the guests at the wedding in Durham House was Dr John Dee (1527-1608), who had acted as tutor to both the bridegrooms. Dee was one of the outstanding intellects of the period, destined to survive the reign of Mary and to emerge as 'Elizabeth's magician'(see page 31). Having struggled to preserve valuable books threatened with destruction during the Reformation and subsequently extended his search throughout the Continent, he had one of the finest libraries of the time. His interests ranged over the fields of mathematics, cartography, astronomy, navigation, surveying and geology and he played a major part in bringing the 'new learning' from the Continent to England.

Like many of his colleagues, however, Dee was also interested in what would now be called magic. The term was indeed applied by many of his contemporaries to the mathematical work in which he was so deeply involved. He studied astrology – the link between celestial and terrestrial events – believing that it could be used to make predictions and hoping that, by using

Dr John Dee. (Courtesy of the Royal College of Physicians)

mirrors and lenses, astral forces could be trapped and utilised. He was a student of the cabbala, a combination of language, mathematics and mythology based on Hebrew, through which, it was supposed, the secrets of the universe would be revealed. He has indeed been nominated as the founder of the English Rosicrucian movement, a secret brotherhood supposedly entrusted with occult wisdom handed down through the ages. But in noting these interests one has to remember that such ideas, which sound ridiculous to modern ears, were once widely entertained by reputable scientists including Newton. In 1647, for example, a Feast of Mathematicians at Gresham College led to the formation of the Society of Astrologers, fifteen years before the Royal Society was incorporated at the same address. Indeed, in recent years it has even been suggested that such studies played a significant part in bringing about the scientific revolution.

Dee's ability to predict and interpret events was utilised by the Queen and the Court, and his familiarity with codes and ciphers may also have been of value to his neighbour, Walsingham, who was in charge of the secret service. His offers to use his occult powers to find buried treasure or to detect mineral deposits were less enthusiastically received, but to Elizabethan seafarers intent on discovering the north-west passage to Cathay (China) his knowledge of navigation and of maps was invaluable, for up to the middle of the sixteenth century the few maps and globes available had been obtained (with difficulty) from the Continent. Dee, moreover, was well aware of the extent of past English explorations and when the Pope suggested that America should be divided between Spain and Portugal he was quick to point out that much of the country was part of an embryonic British Empire.

Towards the end of Elizabeth's reign, the concept of astrology became unpopular and it was therefore easy for Essex to stir up feeling against his rival Sir Walter Raleigh (now living in Durham House), a 'school of night' over which he presided and his 'magician' – commonly supposed to be John Dee. Dee's house and library were destroyed and virtually all that has survived of one of England's great thinkers is a cache of soggy manuscripts dug up near the site of his home by Sir Robert Cotton, and some papers recovered from a secret compartment in a desk by Elias Ashmole.

THE ADELPHI

By 1600 Durham House was in a state of decline. The Earl of Salisbury, Robert Cecil, had incorporated part of the eastern side of the site into the gardens of Salisbury House (not to be confused with the Salisbury House near St Bride's) and in 1608, when the northern part of Durham House was destroyed by fire, it was replaced by the New Exchange, a department store (reputedly 'greatly superior to those in Paris') designed by Inigo Jones. Plans to rebuild the rest of the site were however aborted by the Civil War and by 1660 it was covered with poor, dilapidated housing.

This, then, was the site chosen for the Adelphi (the Greek word for brothers) by the Scottish architects, the Adam brothers. Built between 1772 and 1774 as a rebellion against the hitherto dominant Palladian style, it was modelled on the waterfront palace of Diocletian at Spalato on the Adriatic. The centrepiece of the scheme was a terrace of eleven magnificent houses set on a series of great arches above a riverside quay. Generally accepted as one of the finest developments

Above: Durham House and its neighbours. (Courtesy of the Guildhall Library, London)

Right: The Strand entrance to Durham House. (Courtesy of the Guildhall Library, London)

The Adelphi terrace. Note the water tower on the left. (Courtesy of the Guildhall Library, London)

in London, it was not built without difficulty. There was a dispute between the Government and the local authority as to who owned the foreshore; customers were reluctant to hire the storage space under the arches because the quay tended to flood at high tide; and the housing, although excellent in itself, was no longer in the most fashionable part of town. Nevertheless, it attracted a succession of distinguished residents, including Garrick, D'Oyly Carte, Bernard Shaw and 'Dr' James Graham.

James Graham (1745-1794), the son of an Edinburgh saddler, studied medicine at Edinburgh. He never qualified but after leaving university he visited America (where he met Franklin and developed an interest in electrical treatments) and Europe before working in Bristol and Bath. Encouraged by his success – for his distinguished patients included people like Georgiana, Duchess of Devonshire – he then established his Temple of Health in the Adelphi. Modestly claiming that 'by air, by magnetism, by musical sounds, by subtile, cordial and balsamic medicines and chemical energy and by positive and negative electricity arbitrarily used I have, as it were, an absolute command over the health, functions and diseases of the human body', he was, as one might have expected, able without fail to effect the most miraculous cures. He certainly saw a large number of patients but it was his lecture-demonstrations (largely devoted to sexual matters) that attracted most attention. These sessions, which featured scantily clad 'goddesses of health' (one of whom was later to become Emma, Lady Hamilton) made full use of lights, music, smells, illusions and unexpected electric shocks and were said (by Graham) to have attracted 'an overflow of at least nine hundred ladies and gentlemen' (a less biased observer counted an audience of eighteen). His most famous product, however, was his Grand Celestial Bed wherein, on payment of a fee of £50, those troubled by impotence or infertility could wallow in music, purple satin, Arabian spices and an electromagnetic field in the certainty that, while they enjoyed 'superior ecstasy', immediate conception would take place. Sadly, the demand for such services proved to be limited and, despite moving to less expensive accommodation, Graham eventually became bankrupt. He was incarcerated in Newgate and subsequently (after adding a sort of evangelical Christianity to his armamentarium) became an itinerant.

Behind the main riverside terrace were more rows of elegant streets, some named after the four *adelphi*, the brothers Robert, John, James and William. But the main terrace, apart from one building at the south-west end, has now been demolished along with most of the houses in the streets behind. At the end of John Adam Street (in which the present-day Durham House bears a plaque commemorating the cartoonist Rowlandson) there is, however, one important survivor, No. 7 Adam Street. This was for many years the headquarters of *The Lancet*, a journal founded in 1823 by a young surgeon called Thomas Wakley (1795-1862). Wakley seems always to have been embroiled in conflicts of one sort or another. In 1820, three years after he qualified, he was (incorrectly) identified as the masked man who deftly decapitated the five Cato Street conspirators after their execution. As a result, he was attacked by their supporters and his house in Argyll Street was destroyed – a series of events that brought him into contact with another reformer and target of the Cato Street gang, William Cobbett, who encouraged Wakley to embark on his celebrated crusades against the medical profession. It is difficult, in the space available, even to list Wakley's many forays and it will suffice to say that at various times he attacked almost every

Above left: The only remaining part of the Adelphi terrace – which can be seen beyond the cab in the previous picture.

Above right: No. 7 Adam Street, once the home of *The Lancet*.

branch of 'the establishment'. Consultants in teaching hospitals were scarified for the nepotistic appointment of incompetent relatives, for the misuse of charitable funds, for the exploitation of students and for experimenting on those who came to them for treatment. The College of Surgeons was attacked for altering its byelaws so as to attain a monopoly on the teaching of anatomy. The 'Old Hags of Rhubarb Hall' – the Society of Apothecaries – and others were criticised for the impurity and uselessness of their drugs. The House of Commons (of which he became a member) was trounced for its handling of the problem of human dissection (of which Wakley thought there was far too much) and for its cynical decision to eliminate grave-robbery by using the bodies of the poor. The workhouses from which these bodies came were denounced as 'antechambers to the grave'. Even the Queen (who used chloroform during childbirth) and the Poet Laureate attracted adverse comment.

Because of these diatribes, the early years of *The Lancet* were, as might be expected, somewhat turbulent. But the journal has always been closely linked with this district and it was in Norfolk Street that Astley Cooper discovered Wakley 'pirating' the lectures he gave at St Thomas's and Guy's for the early editions. On the whole, publishers were not eager to be associated with a journal that made regular appearances in the courts, but for some years *The Lancet* was printed in Bolt Court (home of the Society in Bolt Court – see pages 81-83) by the firm Mills, Jowett and Mills – Jowett being the father of the famous Master of Balliol. In 1836 Wakely moved to Essex Street where, perhaps of necessity, he took over both editing and printing himself, and eleven years later he moved to Bedford Street on the opposite side of the Strand. This was the home of *The Lancet* until 1929, when it moved to the Adelphi.

Although the Adelphi has lost virtually all its original housing, the underworld of the Adelphi remains intact. The gardens of Durham House sloped down steeply towards the river and because of this the area had to be built up to create a level site. This produced a vast complex of underground cellars, passages and roads, most of which are still there. At various times they have been used as a stable for cattle and horses, as a playground by Charles Dickens and as a haunt for crooks and prostitutes. There is, for example, a corner called Jenny's Hole, where a Victorian prostitute was murdered in her 'squat', and a trapdoor that once led from a stable up into the basement of a fine house owned by a highwayman. There are underground roads like Lower Robert Street, which is still open, where for many years firms of wine merchants, precision engineers and locksmiths had their premises. At one time there was even a tumbledown riverside pub, the Fox-under-the-Hill, that may be the place where Copperfield met the Micawbers 'in a protruding wooden room which over-hung the river'. Many of these streets have now become part of the Savoy car park but the old wine cellar, which stretches from the Savoy towards Charing Cross station, was converted into a bar called Heaven under the Arches.

THE EMBANKMENT

The idea of confining the Thames by building an embankment was not new, for it had already been suggested by (among others) Christopher Wren and by Pepys' medical friend Sir William Petty. Nothing, however, had been done and by the middle of the nineteenth century the Thames, the ultimate repository for all the refuse and sewage from a greatly enlarged city, was still wide and sluggish – so sluggish that instead of being carried away by the tide its filthy contents just drifted to and fro, constantly churned up by the blades of paddle steamers. But unbeknown to the citizens there was a second, more sinister, problem. In an attempt to improve the supply of water, pumps and towers – like the one near the York Watergate – had been installed at several points along the river. These certainly increased the quantity of water

Above: Lower Robert Street, under the Adelphi.

Right: The Fox under the Hill. (Courtesy of the Guildhall Library, London)

available but, as it was drawn directly from what was in effect the main sewer, its quality left much to be desired. Moreover, the abundance of water encouraged householders to fit the new water closets, an 'improvement' which, without disposing of over 200,000 cesspits and improving the primitive drainage system, was a recipe for disaster. Cesspits, for all their faults, did limit the spread of sewage but they were not designed to contain the discharge from innumerable water closets. Consequently, as Snow had predicted, the introduction of the latter resulted in a wholesale escape of sewage into the water supply. But simply removing the cesspits without altering the system of drainage merely deposited more sewage in the river, as a result of which fish and swans, hitherto plentiful, disappeared. Indeed, as early as 1827 Parliament had been expressly warned that the pipes of the Chelsea Water Company were 'charged with the contents of the great common sewers, the drainings from dunghills and laystalls, the refuse from hospitals, slaughterhouses, colour, lead and soap works, drug mills and factories and all sorts of decomposing animal and vegetable substances'. But although Chadwick, secretary to the newly created General Board of Health, toyed with the idea of uniting the water companies and drawing supplies from Surrey, he and influential figures such as Florence Nightingale were still preoccupied with a belief that illness was due to a 'miasma' that emanated from dirt. Their prime objective was therefore 'the complete purification of dwelling houses, next of the streets and last of the river'. To this end, they directed their energies to washing through the drains and increasing the rate of flow therein, thus ensuring that the river, the main source of drinking water, was even more polluted.

The result was predictable and after further devastating outbreaks of cholera in 1849 and 1854 the Board of Health was replaced by the Metropolitan Board of Works, which directed its energies to cleaning up the Thames. This, however, did not imply that the danger of drinking polluted water had been recognised. Indeed, despite convincing evidence from Snow and others, and even a *Punch* cartoon of a drop of heavily 'infected' Thames water, experts 'could still see no reason to adopt such a belief'. Rather, it was the Great Stink of 1858, which threatened to drive Parliament and the Court out of town, that induced the chief engineer, Bazalgette, to cleanse the Thames by piping all sewage away to the east of the City. The basis of this scheme was a set of large ducts running from west to east that intercepted all other sewers and carried their contents to a pumping station downstream – an operation, undertaken between 1859 and 1865, which involved the use of 318 million bricks and 880,000 cubic yards of concrete. In all, 100 miles of interceptory sewers drained 450 miles of main sewers which in turn were fed by 13,000

A *Punch* illustration of a drop of Thames water.

Right: Sir Joseph Bazalgette.

Below: A view from Hungerford Market, which stood on the site of Hungerford House (destroyed by fire in 1669). Note the York Watergate on the left, the Adelphi, the muddy foreshore reclaimed by the Embankment and the paddle steamer. Hungerford Market was replaced by Charing Cross station. (Courtesy of the Guildhall Library, London)

A section of the Embankment showing the main drain, other services, the Underground line and the site of the new gardens. (Courtesy of the Guildhall Library, London)

miles of smaller sewers. Included in this project was the Thames Embankment that ran for over a mile between Westminster and Blackfriars. This amazing scheme recaptured between 100ft and 400ft of sewage-laden foreshore, housed one of the main interceptory drains and speeded up the rate of flow of the river. It also provided a public garden on the Embankment (whose many adornments included Cleopatra's Needle, the importation of which was largely financed by the surgeon Erasmus Wilson), a bypass for the Strand and Fleet Street and (when the finances had been sorted out) part of the London Underground's Circle Line.

By the time the Embankment was completed, the filtration of drinking water (using a technique devised by the versatile Dr Peter Roget of Thesaurus fame) was being introduced. Even so, it was evident that a project undertaken to abolish the Great Stink had in fact achieved far more, for, as Bazalgette himself observed, 'however occult might be the connection between death and defective drainage, places formerly most favourable to the spread of disease become quite free from it when properly drained'. London's last outbreak of cholera, in 1866, was in a small area of Whitechapel not included in Bazalgette's scheme (an oversight that was revealed when it was discovered that the pipe to a non-functioning tap was blocked by an eel) and thirty years later, when Hamburg (a major trading partner) had another massive outbreak, London was spared.

11

THE CENTRE OF MEDICINE

Hospitals, BMA House and the Epstein Statues

At the peak of its scientific development, the area boasted two teaching hospitals and the headquarters of the Royal College of Surgeons, the British Medical Association and The Lancet. *The way in which the BMA chose to adorn its new building caused a major outcry.*

By the start of the nineteenth century, the structure of medical practice was becoming more clearly defined. Professional organisations were developing and the concentration of illness and injury in England's rapidly growing cities had prompted philanthropists to found a significant number of new hospitals. This was an innovation that the medical profession was happy to support, for apart from enhancing its prestige, 'hospitals furnished by voluntary contribution', as one writer observed, 'tend to promote and perfect knowledge of the art, making the benefits extend to all ranks of people'. The extension, of course, was usually upwards and one German professor stated quite openly that 'the hospital is not there for the benefit of the patient, but the patient for the hospital'. For people like Benjamin Golding, however, the objective was purely philanthropic. Golding, a wealthy medical student who lived near Leicester Square, was horrified by the indescribable filth and wretchedness he saw around his home. In 1815 he was therefore moved to open his house daily 'to such poor persons as desire gratuitous advice'. This led in 1818 to the foundation of the little West London Infirmary and Dispensary behind the Haymarket Theatre. In 1823 the hospital moved to No. 28 Villiers Street, to the east of Charing Cross station, and in 1834, having changed its name to the Charing Cross Hospital, it moved to the Decimus Burton building (now a police station) on the opposite side of the Strand. The hospital, whose graduates include David Livingstone, remained on this site until 1973, when it moved to Fulham.

The Charing Cross, however, was not the only teaching hospital associated with the area. Because of the long-standing (and bitterly resented) refusal of Oxford and Cambridge to admit those who were not Anglicans, a new London college, University College, had been founded in 1826. But there was widespread alarm when it was discovered that, in addition to accepting Dissenters, this 'godless College of Gower Street' would not teach divinity. A movement was therefore started to provide a more wholesome alternative in which, while the religious beliefs of the students were still immaterial, the staff (which included Lord Lister, Herbert Mayo – formerly a pupil of Sir Charles Bell, who had claimed credit for discoveries about the function of the fifth and seventh cranial nerves made by his subordinate – and Charles Leyell, Professor of Geology, whose book *Principles of Geology* was 'of the highest service' to Darwin on the *Beagle* expedition)

The old Charing Cross
Hospital, Strand.

were members of the Church of England. The welfare of the students was nevertheless a matter
of great concern, and when a site to the east of Somerset House was chosen it was pointed out
that 'from a moral point of view it was probably the very worst that could have been selected
in the whole metropolis, being within about a five minutes' walk of five theatres'. Moreover,
despite obtaining the backing of the Prime Minister (the Duke of Wellington) and the patronage
of the King, the project nearly foundered over Wellington's support of Catholic Emancipation.
This argument became so heated that the Duke challenged one of his critics to a duel, but
eventually the problems were resolved and the architect, Sir Robert Smirke, was left with the
difficult and expensive task of completing the eastern end of Chambers' design for Somerset
House on an unstable sloping riverside site. King's College finally opened in 1831 and among
its various departments was one that taught medicine. Eight years later, by upgrading the St
Clement Danes workhouse in Portugal Street on the opposite side of the Strand, it acquired
a hospital and this was subsequently enlarged and rebuilt to produce what – at the time – was
regarded as one of the most modern hospitals in London. It closed when the King's College
Hospital moved to Denmark Hill in 1913 and the site is marked by a plaque halfway along the
south side of Portugal Street.

THE 'LONDON BURKERS'

The building of King's College, Somerset House had barely been completed when, in 1831, it
was the scene of a horrifying discovery. At that time, the only legitimate source of bodies for
dissection was judicial execution, for under the 1752 Murder Act those guilty of particularly vile
crimes could be hanged, dissected in public and denied a burial service. But in London, where
it was estimated that over 1,000 bodies were dissected each year, only a dozen were available
from this source. The rest, as has been explained above (page 85), were simply stolen and even
a new building like King's College had a room where 'resurrectionists' could be received. The
authorities were of course aware of what was going on but, because doctors had to be trained,
they shied away from the difficult task of designating bodies for this purpose. Instead they

Above: The old King's College Hospital, Portugal Street. (Courtesy of the Guildhall Library, London)

Right: Plaque in Portugal Street marking the site of King's College Hospital.

simply ignored the wholesale looting of hospital mortuaries and the importation of bodies from elsewhere, provided cadavers from the great military hospitals and dealt lightly with grave-robbers. The public, by contrast, was strongly opposed to such activities and did everything in its power to frustrate them. So successful were these efforts that, coupled with new judicial rulings that even receiving a stolen body was a punishable offence, the supply of bodies was curtailed and many students were forced to study abroad where cadavers were more readily available.

It was therefore evident that, if the teaching of anatomy was to continue, new legislation was required and it was probably Abernethy who, in 1819, first suggested that the bodies of paupers should be used. There was a certain logic in this, for it was from grossly overcrowded pauper burial grounds (like the one near the St Clement Danes Workhouse in Portugal Street) that many of the bodies currently being used were obtained. Moreover, there was a feeling – soon to be enshrined in the Poor Law Act of 1834 – that the 'undeserving poor' were guilty of some sort of crime. What could be more appropriate than that they should repay their debt to society – with their bodies? It was of course possible for paupers to 'opt out' – if they were literate and knew the regulations. Similarly, relatives or friends could claim the body – if they could pay for the funeral. But many faced the prospect of an ignominious fate hitherto reserved for the worst sort of murderer.

The first Bill to Prevent the Unlawful Disinterment of Human Bodies and for Regulating Schools of Anatomy was drawn up by a carefully selected committee and eased through the Commons with a skill that earned it the sobriquet of the Midnight Bill. It was defeated in the Lords. But in the meantime a new horror had come to light. It was known that, in Scotland, Burke and Hare (who were not grave-robbers) had been supplying anatomists with the bodies of people they had murdered. Bentham had indeed warned the Prime Minister that unless something was done about the situation the same thing would happen in England. It had.

At noon on Saturday 5 November 1831 three men, John Bishop, James May and Thomas Williams, visited the Department of Anatomy at King's College to ask the porter if he wanted a body. (This was a common practice – St Bartholomew's even kept a supply of hampers for such 'salesmen' to use.) But William Hill, the Dissecting Room porter, was unhappy about the cadaver they produced – that of a young man who appeared to have died recently and did not seem to have been buried. He therefore summoned the Demonstrator in Anatomy, Richard Partridge, who contrived to detain the vendors by claiming that he would have to get change for a £50 note before he could pay them. Ten minutes later he returned with the police, who arrested the three 'London Burkers'. A month later Bishop and Head were hanged, Bishop's skeleton joining the other exhibits in the King's College Museum. May, destined for Botany Bay, died before his ship left the Thames. The unfortunate Hill was driven out of his job – ostensibly because other resurrectionists refused to do business with him.

The resulting outcry renewed the demand for legislation and, under cover of the Reform Bill, a revised Anatomy Act was introduced. It was carefully worded, emotive terms like 'dissection' and 'graveyard' being avoided, but its objective remained the same. Indeed, as the peer who introduced it to the Upper House rather naively observed, 'it would be an improvement if the provisions could be so framed as not to point out so disturbingly that its operation has reference to one particular class'. The Bill had many other defects, not least the obligation to provide a Christian burial – a regulation which, as recent events have shown, left some doubt as to whether anatomists could retain specimens. But, propelled by the crime discovered at King's College, the Act became law in 1832.

BMA HOUSE

In addition to two teaching hospitals, however, there were two professional organisations situated in or near the Strand. The surgeons (now the Royal College of Surgeons) had moved to Lincoln's Inn Fields in 1798 – an event which horrified the residents, who did not relish the idea of neighbours who spent their time dismembering bodies. In fact, they need not have worried, for it transpired that the cadavers to which the surgeons were entitled had to be dissected within 400 yards of Newgate. The surgeons were therefore obliged to rent a nearby building – No. 33 Hosier Lane – just beyond the Fortunes of War, the public house which was the body-snatchers' headquarters. It was here that the bodies of Bishop and Head, the 'London Burkers', were received and ceremonially opened in the presence of the City Marshal, the president of the College of Surgeons (fully robed) and his colleagues. Only then could they be presented to the anatomists. But the new building in Lincoln's Inn Fields was soon to become the home of the great anatomical collection built by John Hunter – his brother's collection, previously offered and refused, having gone to Glasgow.

At the other end of the Strand, opposite Charing Cross station, was the headquarters of another medical organisation whose conduct was about to horrify its neighbours, the British Medical Association. The BMA was growing rapidly and the general secretary, rightly anticipating a need for a larger building, had been prudently buying up adjoining houses and land so that, by 1902, it was possible to erect a new building on the same site. The architect chosen for this venture was an innovative young man called Charles Holden, later to become famous for the design of the Senate House of London University and of some fifty Underground stations. It was his idea that the lower part of the new building should be built of granite and the top three storeys in Portland stone, the two sections being linked by a frieze of eighteen life-size statues, also carved in Portland stone but thrown into contrast by being set against the top of the granite section. It was an idea that appealed to the worthies of the BMA, who had in mind a set of carvings of great figures from the history of medicine. This, however, was not what was intended by the sculptor, a young man called Jacob Epstein, for whom this was to be his first major commission. He wanted to portray the seven ages of man and the spiritual and physical energy of life in a series of figures that were 'joyous, energetic, mystical' – and nude. This being so, as he pointed out, 'surgeons with side whiskers, no matter how eminent, could hardly serve my purpose'. It was therefore with some diffidence that he appeared before the planning committee, only to find, to his delight, that his scheme was accepted virtually without alteration. In the summer of 1907, great blocks of Portland stone were therefore hauled up onto the front of the building and the sculptor began to work in situ from a series of models.

All went well until the following June, when a lady working in an office in the Nash pepperpot opposite looked out of her window and saw, silhouetted against the London skyline, a naked, heavily pregnant woman gazing down at her distended abdomen. This was the model of Maternity, who was meant to be looking at a child in her arms, which unfortunately had not yet

The old headquarters of the British Medical Association, Strand.

Epstein's 'Maternity' (without child).

been delivered from the studio. Even more unfortunately, the lady concerned – that is the one in the office – worked for the National Vigilance Association, the Mary Whitehouse organisation of its day. Immediately there was pandemonium. A reporter from the *Evening Standard* hurried to the Strand and declared the carvings 'a scandal'. Crowds (mainly of young women) gathered in the street to see what little they could. Father Bernard Vaughan, 'without some platitude from whom no public discussion would ever be complete', as the BMJ observed, deplored this attempt to 'convert London to a Fiji island' with statues that would 'occasion vulgar and unwholesome talk'. Even the chairman of the Council of the BMA was quoted as saying that the statues 'should never have been put there'.

Work came to an abrupt halt, but over the next few days it became evident that Epstein also had his backers. Leading figures from the world of arts wrote giving their support and *The Times* urged the BMA not to give way to the 'hypocrisy and Philistinism of a portion of our middle class'. There was even a clerical counterblast from the Bishop of Stepney, Cosmo Gordon Lang ('old Lang swine' of the abdication crisis) who, after climbing up to view the statues at close quarters, found 'nothing indecent or shocking'. The Premises Committee, in a meeting which Epstein likened to 'an ancient ecclesiastical court assembled to consider a heresy case', reviewed the situation – and a stack of letters nearly a foot high, including one from the chairman of the Council repudiating the remarks attributed to him – and finally asked the director of the National Gallery for a second opinion.

The conclusion was unequivocal. The statues were deemed to be 'too severe and reverent to be in any way improper' and the assessor added, 'I believe that in the future, when he has made a name for himself that this work promises, the British Medical Association will be proud to have given this young man this commission'. The statues remained. It was not long, however, before they were once more at the centre of a dispute. In 1925 the BMA moved to Tavistock Square, the old headquarters became Rhodesia House, and word leaked out that the statues, which were 'not perhaps within the austerity usually appertaining to government buildings', were to be removed. Once more the world of arts rose in wrath, and in the face of this onslaught the new owners again left them where they were. But the respite was brief, for there was another more serious problem. The Portland stone had weathered badly and a few years later, during the removal of bunting tied to one of the statues for the Coronation of George VI, a piece fell off and caused a minor injury to a pedestrian. Immediately scaffolding was erected, the statues were carefully inspected and any potentially dangerous parts were ruthlessly hacked off. The line of statues that adorns what is now Zimbabwe House is therefore but a shadow of its former self – a feeble reminder of the days when the Strand was surrounded by the College of Surgeons, two teaching hospitals and the headquarters of the BMA and *The Lancet*.

Remains of the Epstein statues, BMA House. The mother and child are on the right.

12

ST BRIDE'S CHURCH

It is not easy, in the bustle of a modern city, to sense the mantle of history that hangs over this part of London. But on a dark Sunday evening, when Fleet Street is quiet, one can perhaps imagine a torch over the entrance to Crane Court advertising a meeting of the Royal Society, Fothergill and his distinguished colleagues feasting at the Mitre or Quakers from Lettsom's dispensaries in earnest conference in Bolt Court. Let your mind go still further back as you cross the road and walk, as Wolsey, Pepys, Johnson, Goldsmith and many others have done, past the site of Milton's house and into St Bride's. The walls and steeple are as Wren built them but the interior, rid of its dark glass and Victorian clutter during an air raid on 29 December 1940, has been gloriously restored after the manner of a college chapel. Stay for Evensong, where a handful of people enjoy music which, in the intimacy of this little church, far surpasses that of the great cathedrals. Look at the lectern, rescued from the Great Fire of 1666 and again in 1940, watch the members of the ancient guild and listen to the words of Evening Prayer, almost unchanged since Cranmer (Henry VIII's supporter) distilled them from the seven offices of the medieval Church. Finally, go down the staircase to the right of the entrance. Here in the crypt you can see the scorch marks on the fifteenth-century building that Wren replaced and the remains of six previous churches, the earliest a Celtic foundation which predates Augustine and the Synod of Whitby. There are Saxon and Roman graves, a Roman ditch and a piece of Roman pavement. Hidden from view there is also a charnel house, sealed up during the cholera epidemic of 1854 when Parliament forbade further burials within the City and rediscovered when the church was restored after the war. It contains around 7,000 human bones gradually removed from the graveyard and neatly stacked according to type, and around 300 coffins whose plates allow the age and sex of the occupant to be identified, making this one of the largest and most valuable collections of its kind. Among them is one believed to be that of Wynkyn de Worde, the printer who, 500 years ago, brought the press to Fleet Street. Here, then, in this ancient crypt, one has a tangible reminder of the days when the Church was indeed 'school, moral tutor, local government and, not least, magic and medicine', and of the historic value of this part of London.

Opposite left: The interior of the restored church. Note the lectern, saved from the fires of 1666 and 1940. (Courtesy of St Bride's church, Fleet Street)

Opposite far right: A view from the tower, taken during restoration, showing the remains of six earlier churches. (Courtesy of St Bride's church, Fleet Street)

Wren's St Bride's, Fleet Street. Salisbury Court is on the right. (Courtesy of St Bride's church, Fleet Street)

The crypt, discovered during restoration, with a coffin and stacks of bones. (Courtesy of St Bride's church, Fleet Street)

Opposite page: 'A building at the College of Physicians designed by Sir Christopher Wren and destroyed by fire in 1897'. The only work Wren is known to have done for the College was to 'make alterations to the new building [at Warwick Lane] to accommodate the [Dorchester] library'. As a teenager in the house of Sir Charles Scarburgh, Wren had watched the designing of the Webb library at Amen Corner, which was destroyed in the Great Fire, and this building is thought to have been the inspiration for his own library at Trinity College, Cambridge, built in 1685. But while Webb's library had square windows on the first floor and arched entrances to the colonnade, in both Wren's buildings this pattern was reversed. Perhaps the library at Warwick Lane – built in 1680 – was a prototype for the one at Cambridge. (Courtesy of the Guildhall Library, London)

13

THE LIBRARY OF THE ROYAL COLLEGE
OF PHYSICIANS

As the proceeds of this book are to go towards the restoration of volumes in the library of the College of Physicians, readers may be interested to know where the College and its library fit into this story.

The physicians were unique in that, unlike other groups (including the surgeons and the apothecaries), they were not governed by one of the City guilds. Founded by Henry VIII in 1518, their College had its first home in a house in Knightrider Street, south of St Paul's. Initially the few books they owned were kept in a chest but in 1614, when the College moved to new premises in Amen Corner to the west of the cathedral, they acquired a set of bookcases. The possibility of a purpose-built library was first raised by the president in 1651. This came as

something of a surprise, for the predominantly Royalist College had been under considerable pressure during the Civil War and the Commonwealth. It transpired, however, that the donor was William Harvey, faithful physician to Charles I, who had been stripped of his hospital posts, heavily fined and banished from London because of this association. The planning of this library must have been watched with interest by the young Christopher Wren, son of the deposed Dean of Windsor, who had found refuge in the home of Sir Charles Scarburgh (Scarburgh, whose near death by drowning was recorded by Pepys – see page 49 – was one of many Royalist physicians whose professional value ensured that they continued to prosper during the Commonwealth. With the Restoration he therefore hastened to greet the new monarch and to name a star in his honour). This presumably explains why the Wren library at Trinity College, Cambridge bears so strong a resemblance to Harvey's library in Amen Corner.

The library, along with the rest of the College, was destroyed in the Great Fire. This, of course, was inevitable but it seems rather strange that only about 100 of the books were saved. There were, after all, members of staff living on the premises and the fire took three or four days to reach this part of the City – during which time the neighbouring apothecaries had removed all their treasures. One wonders if the refusal to go on paying the librarian (whose absence during the plague had already occasioned one serious loss) implies that there were others who felt that he might have done more to preserve the property of the College.

The new College, whose domed lecture theatre reminded one observer of 'a distant vision of a gilded pill', was designed by Robert Hooke and built opposite the Old Bailey in Warwick Lane. (It was this building that was stormed by the Licentiates – see pages 79-80) It was of course virtually devoid of books but steps were being taken to remedy this deficiency. The College had already met the Marquis of Dorchester, a friend and patient of William Harvey. Dorchester, a noted bibliophile, had a great interest in medicine and had already given £100 to Harvey's library at Amen Corner. A year later, in 1657, we find Wren at Dorchester's home trying (without success) to demonstrate his latest experiment, the injection of an emetic into the veins of a dog, and a year after that Dorchester was made an Honorary Fellow of the College. The contact was obviously maintained, for after the Great Fire Dorchester's new physician, Edward Browne (whose home in Crane Court was bought by the Royal Society – see page 70) was probably instrumental in arranging that his library of some 2,000 volumes – reputedly the best in private hands in England – was left to the College. Among its many treasures were over 100 books that had clearly been stolen from the library of John Dee (see page 97). To house this collection, Wren was asked to modify the new building.

In 1825, because of the social and professional decline of the City, the College moved to a new building (now the Canadian Embassy) on the west side of Trafalgar Square. This was not a memorable period in its history but the site was close to the newly founded Athenaeum – an organisation to which many of the Fellows belonged and which catered for 'Gentlemen who have published some literary or professional work ... although bishops and judges might be admitted whether they have published or not'. In 1964 the College moved yet again, to its present home in Regent's Park. By this time, the library had amassed many treasures, ranging from individual volumes (some bearing the armorial bindings of Queen Elizabeth, the Earl of Leicester, Francis Bacon and, of course, the Marquis of Dorchester) to important collections – including one that was awaiting removal by the local refuse department when it was tracked down and rescued by a Fellow of the College.

It would be impossible, in the space available, to describe the scale or the importance of the library as it stands today. But if one had to point out one item to those studying an area whose reputation is largely dependent on the printed word, it would perhaps be a 1473 edition of St Augustine's book *The City of God*, a volume that was once in the Imperial Library at St

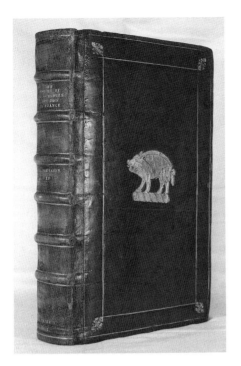

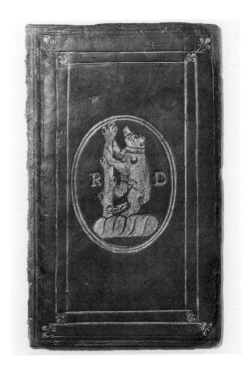

Volumes from the library of the Royal College of Physicians bearing the emblems of the original owners – the boar (Francis Bacon), the bear and staff (Robert Dudley) and the fox (the Marquis of Dorchester). (Courtesy of the Royal College of Physicians)

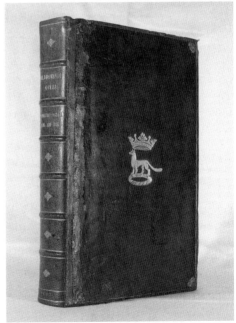

Petersburg. It comes from a time in which virtually every book was written out by hand, as a result of which no two copies were identical. Because of this, at least one publisher, whose customers had discovered that this was not so, had been charged with sorcery. As a precaution, the publisher of this volume therefore added a note explaining that it had been produced by a new technique called printing.

CHRONOLOGY

Roman pavement, Saxon graves.

c. 500   First St Bride's church built
1162   The Knights Templar move to Fleet Street
c.1237   York House built for the Bishops of Norwich
c.1250   Foundation of Whitefriars Monastery
1278   Foundation of Blackfriars Monastery
13th century   Building of Arundel House (Bishops of Bath and Wells), Durham House, Essex House (Bishops of Exeter) and Savoy Palace
1375   Guild of St Bride founded
14th century   Foundation of Inns of Court
(*1492   Columbus' voyage to America*)
1500   Wynkyn de Worde moves to Fleet Street
1505   Building of the Savoy Hospital
1509   Henry VIII becomes King
1515   Restoration of the Bridewell Palace
1525   Birth of Roderigo Lopez (1525-1594)
1527   Birth of John Dee (1527-1608)
1529   Henry VIII's divorce hearing in Blackfriars
1534   The break with Rome
1545   Arundel House rebuilt by Thomas Seymour
1547   Edward VI becomes King
1549   Execution of Thomas Seymour; Cranmer's *Book of Common Prayer* printed.
c.1550   Copperplate map of London produced
1552   Execution of 'Protector' Somerset; birth of Simon Forman (1552-1611)
1553   Mary becomes Queen; foundation of Bridewell Hospital; execution of Northumberland and Lady Jane Grey; birth of Thomas Moffett (1553-1604)
1558   Elizabeth I becomes Queen
1561   Birth of Francis Bacon (1561-1626)
1563   Earl of Leicester restores Essex House
1586   Death of Philip Sidney

(*1588   Spanish Armada*)
c. 1590   Norden's map of London produced
1601   Execution of second Earl of Essex
1603   James I becomes King
1604   Building of Salisbury House in the Strand, on part of the Durham House site
1608   Building of New Exchange on part of the Durham House site
1610   Building of Prince Henry's Room
1616   Visscher's map of London produced
1618   Publication of *London Pharmacopoeia*
(*1620   The Pilgrim Fathers set sail for America*)
1625   Charles I becomes King
1626   York Watergate built
1628   Murder of the Duke of Buckingham (1592-1628)
1632   Building of Apothecaries' Hall at Blackfriars; Birth of Samuel Pepys (1632-1703)
1640   Birth of Nicholas Barbon (1640-1698)
1649   Execution of Charles I; start of the Commonwealth
1649   Culpeper's *Physical Directory* published
1658   Hollar's drawing of west London produced
1660   Charles II becomes King; demolition of Durham House.
1662   Incorporation of the Royal Society; publication of Graunt's study of the Bills of Mortality
1665   The Great Plague
1666   The Great Fire; the Royal Society moves to Arundel House
1667   First transfusion in England at Arundel House; Bridewell rebuilt
1668   Apothecaries' Hall rebuilt
1670   Demolition of York House
1673   The Royal Society returns to Gresham College
1674   Demolition of Essex House; St Bride's church rebuilt
1678   Demolition of Arundel House
1685   James II becomes King
1689   William and Mary become King and Queen
1691   Building of the river steps from the terrace of the old Whitehall Palace; York water tower constructed
1694   William III becomes King
1702   Anne becomes Queen
1709   Birth of Samuel Johnson (1709-1784)
1712   The Royal Society moves to Crane Court
1714   George I becomes King.
1727   George II becomes King.
1728   Birth of Oliver Goldsmith (1728-1774)
1733 and 1766   Fleet river enclosed
1739   Birth of William Hewson (1739-1774)
1745   Birth of James Graham (1745-1794)
1749   Bucks' map of London produced
1752   Foundation of the Society of Physicians
1760   George III becomes King
1767   Foundation of the Society of Collegiate Physicians

(*1768-1779   Cook's voyages*)
1769   Building of Blackfriars Bridge
1773   Foundation of the Society in Crane Court
1774   Durham House replaced by the Adelphi
1775   Rebuilding of Somerset House; (*American War of Independence 1775-1781*)
1776   Destruction of Savoy Hospital.
1780   The Royal Society moves to Somerset House
1786   The Society in Crane Court moves to Bolt Court
1795   Birth of Thomas Wakley (1795-1862)
1798   The Royal College of Surgeons moves to Lincoln's Inn Fields
1803   Foundation of the Royal Jennerian Society, Salisbury Court
(*1805   Battle of Trafalgar*)
1817   Building of Waterloo Bridge
1820   George IV becomes King
1823   West London Hospital moves to Villiers Street
1830   William IV becomes King.
1831   Opening of King's College; first cholera epidemic
1834   Opening of Charing Cross Hospital in the Strand
1837   Victoria becomes Queen
1839   Foundation of King's College Hospital
1841   Construction of Brunel's Hungerford Suspension Bridge
1848   Second cholera epidemic
1850   The Society in Bolt Court moves to the West End
1854   The crypt of St Bride's church sealed after third cholera epidemic; destruction of Hungerford Market; (*Crimean War and Indian Mutiny 1854-1856*)
1857   The Royal Society moves to Burlington House
1858   The Great Stink
1864   Building of Charing Cross station; construction of the Embankment 1864-1870
1878   Cleopatra's Needle erected
1895   Discovery of Whitefriars Monastery crypt
(*Boer War 1899-1902*)
1901   Edward VII becomes King
1908   The Epstein Statues crisis
1910   George V becomes King
1913   King's College Hospital moves to Denmark Hill
(*First World War 1914-1918*)
1925   Closure of the BMA offices in the Strand.
1929   *The Lancet* moves to the Adelphi.
1936   Edward VIII becomes King then abdicates; George VI becomes King
1937   Rebuilding of Waterloo Bridge
(*Second World War 1939-1945*)
1940   Destruction of St Bride's church.
1952   Elizabeth II becomes Queen
1957   Opening of the new (eighth) St Bride's church
1973   Charing Cross Hospital leaves the Strand
1985   Departure of the newspapers from Fleet Street

BIBLIOGRAPHY

It has been emphasised in the preface that this book is not based on original study but on material collected from many different sources. In a work intended for the general reader it would not be appropriate to give every reference used. I have, however, relied heavily on the following books and articles, which would be of interest to anyone who wished to study the subject in greater detail.

Ackroyd, P., *London: The Biography*, Chatto & Windus, 2000.

Barker, F. and P. Jackson, *London: 2,000 Years of a City and its People,* Cassell, 1974.

Booth, C., 'Doctors in Science and Society', *British Medical Journal*, 1987.

Bryant, A., *Samuel Pepys – Man in the Making, Years of Peril, Saviour of the Navy*, Collins, 1933.

Chapman, H.W., *The Last Tudor King,* Cape, 1961.

Fraser, A., *The Six Wives of Henry VIII,* Weidenfeld and Nicholson, 1992.

Green, D., *The Double Life of Doctor Lopez*, Century London, 2003.

Griffin, J.P., 'London's medieval hospitals and the Reformation', *Journal of the Royal College of Physicians*, 1998, Vol.32, p.72.

Heron, J.R., 'Bold statues on the BMA building', *British Medical Journal*, 1980, Vol.2, p.1710.

Hibbert, C.C., *London: The Biography of a City*, Penguin, 1980.

Hunter, M., *Science and Society in Restoration England*, Gregg Revivals, 1992.

Hunting, P., *The Medical Society of London 1773-2003*, Medical Society of London, 2004.

Jardine, L., *On a Grander Scale: The Outstanding Career of Sir Christopher Wren*, Harper Collins, 2002.

Jardine, L., *Ingenious Pursuits*, Little Brown, 1999.

Jardine, L. and A. Stewart, *Hostage to Fortune: The Troubled Life of Francis Bacon,* Weidenfeld and Nicholson, 1998.

Kilpatrick, R., 'Living in the light' in *Medical Enlightenment in the Eighteenth Century*, A. Cunningham (ed.), Cambridge, 1990.

Knapman, P., 'Benjamin Franklin and the Craven Street Bones', *Transactions of the Medical Society of London 1999-2000*, Vol.116, p.9.

Lacey R., *Robert, Earl of Essex – An Elizabethan Icarus*, Weidenfeld and Nicholson, 1971.

Lyons, J.B., *The Mystery of Oliver Goldsmith's Medical Degree*, Carraig Books, Dublin, 1978.

Mason, A.S., 'Little Miss Muffet's Father', *Journal of the Royal College of Physicians* 1993, Vol.27, p.322.

Morgan, D., *Phoenix of Fleet Street: 2000 Years of St Bride's*, Charles Knight, 1973.

Murray, T.J., 'Samuel Johnson: his ills, his pills and his physician friends', *Clinical Medicine* 2003, Vol.3, p.368.

Pevsner, N., *London: Volume 1*, Penguin, 1962.

Porter, R., *London: A Social History*, Penguin, 1996.

Porter, R., *Quacks: Fakers and Charlatans in English Medicine*, Tempus, 2000.

Purver, M., *The Royal Society: Concept and Creation*, Routledge, 1992.

Redworth, G., *The Prince and the Infanta*, Yale, 2003.

Schama, S., *A History of Britain*, BBC, 2000.

Spillane, J.D., *Medical Travellers*, Oxford, 1984.

Starkey, D. et al, *Elizabeth I: The Exhibition Catalogue*, Chatto & Windus 2003.

Stevenson, C., *Medicine and Magnificence: British Hospital Architecture 1660-1815*, Yale University Press, 2000.

Tomalin, C., *Samuel Pepys: The Unequalled Self*, Penguin Viking, 2002.

Traister, B., *The Notorious Astrological Physician of London: The Works and Days of Simon Forman*, University of Chicago Press, 2001.

Trench, R. and E. Hillman, *London under London*, John Murray, 1984.

Weinreb, B. and C. Hibbert, *The London Encyclopaedia*, Macmillan, 1983.

Wilford, N., 'The life and work of William Hewson, haematologist and immunologist' in *Medicine in Northumbria*, Alpha Word Power for the Pybus Society, 1993.

Wilson, D., *The Uncrowned Kings of England: The Black Legend of the Dudleys*, Constable, 2005.

Wise, S., *The Italian Boy: Murder and Grave-robbery in 1830s London*, Cape, 2004.

Woolley, B., *The Queen's Conjuror: The Life and Magic of Dr Dee*, Harper Collins, 2001.

Woolley, B., *The Herbalist: Nicholas Culpeper and the Fight for Medical Freedom*, Harper Collins, 2004.

Zimmer, C., *Soul Made Flesh*, Heinemann, 2004.

INDEX